Physical Characteristics of the Ibizan Hound
(from the American Kennel Club breed standard)

Body: The chest is deep and long with the breastbone sharply angled and prominent. The ribs are slightly sprung. The brisket is approximately 2.5 inches above the elbow. The deepest part of the chest, behind the elbow, is nearly to or to the elbow. The abdomen is well tucked up, but not exaggerated. The loin is very slightly arched, of medium breadth and well muscled. The croup is very slightly sloping.

Tail: Set low, highly mobile, and reaches at least to the hock. It is carried in a sickle, ring, or saber position, according to the mood and individual specimen.

Hindquarters: Angulation is moderate with the hindquarters being set under the body. The thighs are very strong with flat muscling. The hocks are straight when viewed from the rear. Bone is clean and fine. There are no rear dewclaws. The feet are as in front.

Color: White or red, (from light, yellowish-red called "lion" to deep red), solid or in any combination. No color or pattern is preferable to the other.

Coat: There are two types of coat; both untrimmed. *Short—* shortest on head and ears and longest at back of the thighs and under the tail. *Wire-haired—*Can be from one to three inches in length with a possible generous moustache. Both types of coat are hard in texture.

Size: The height of dogs is 23.5 inches to 27.5 inches at the withers. Bitches are 22.5 to 26 inches at the withers. Average weight of dogs is 50 pounds; bitches, 45 pounds.

Ibizan Hound

By Juliette Cunliffe

Contents

8

History of the Ibizan Hound

Travel to the Spanish isle of Ibiza to learn about the beginnings of the Ibizan Hound, as well as its ancestors that were highly valued in ancient Egypt. Discover this sighthound's history as a prized hunting dog in its native land, as well as France. From there, travel to the United Kingdom, the United States and other destinations to uncover the breed's history in show.

18

Characteristics of the Ibizan Hound

Explore the one-of-a-kind personality of the Ibizan Hound. This stunning, elegant hound is quite intelligent, personable and high-energy and possesses chase and escape instincts that will require the right owners to train and care for it. The chapter also discusses the physical characteristics and health concerns of this generally hardy breed.

28

Breed Standard for the Ibizan Hound

Learn the requirements of a well-bred Ibizan Hound by studying the description of the breed set forth in the American Kennel Club standard. Both show dogs and pets must possess key characteristics as outlined in the breed standard.

36

Your Puppy Ibizan Hound

Find out about how to locate a well-bred Ibizan Hound puppy. Discover which questions to ask the breeder and what to expect when visiting the litter. Prepare for your puppy-accessory shopping spree. Also discussed are home safety, the first trip to the vet, socialization and solving basic puppy problems.

63

Proper Care of Your Ibizan Hound

Cover the specifics of taking care of your Ibizan Hound every day: feeding for the puppy, adult and senior dog; grooming, including coat care, ears, eyes, nails and bathing; and exercise needs for your dog. Also discussed are the essentials of dog ID and boarding.

Training Your Ibizan Hound   **83**

Begin with the basics of training the puppy and adult dog. Learn the principles of house-training the Ibizan Hound, including the use of crates and basic scent instincts. Get started by introducing the pup to his collar and leash and progress to the basic commands. Find out about obedience classes and training for other activities.

Healthcare of Your Ibizan Hound   **107**

By Lowell Ackerman DVM, DACVD
Become your dog's healthcare advocate and a well-educated canine keeper. Select a skilled and able veterinarian. Discuss pet insurance, vaccinations and infectious diseases, the neuter/spay decision and a sensible, effective plan for parasite control, including fleas, ticks and worms.

Showing Your Ibizan Hound   **128**

Step into the center ring and find out about the world of showing pure-bred dogs. Here's how to get started in AKC shows, how they are organized and what's required for your dog to become a champion. Take a leap into the realms of obedience trials, agility, tracking tests, lure coursing and racing.

Behavior of Your Ibizan Hound   **146**

Analyze the canine mind to understand what makes your Ibizan Hound tick. The following potential problems are addressed: aggression (fear-biting, inter-canine and dominant), separation anxiety, digging and food-related problems.

Index. 156

KENNEL CLUB BOOKS® **IBIZAN HOUND**
ISBN: 1-59378-389-2

Copyright © 2007 • Kennel Club Books® • A Division of BowTie, Inc.
40 Broad Street, Freehold, NJ 07728 USA
Cover Design Patented: US 6,435,559 B2 • Printed in South Korea

Library of Congress Cataloging-in-Publication Data
Cunliffe, Juliette
  Ibizan hound / by Juliette Cunliffe.
    p. cm. -- (A comprehensive owner's guide ; 186)
  ISBN 1-59378-389-2
  1. Ibizan hound. I. Title.
  SF429.I24C86 2006
  636.753'2--dc22   2006029015

10 9 8 7 6 5 4 3 2 1

Photography by Mary Bloom, Isabelle Français and Juliette Cunliffe with additional photos by:

Carol Beuchat, Paulette Braun, Carolina Biological Supply, Tom Di Giacomo, Karen Giles, Stephen Hall, Carol Ann Johnson, Bill Jonas, Dr. Dennis Kunkel, Ludwig Photography, Tam C. Nguyen, Phototake, Jean Claude Revy, Sanne Rutloh, Jay Singh, Luis Sosa, Susan & Lennah, Chuck Tatham and Christina Timbury.

Illustrations by Patricia Peters.

The publisher would like to thank all owners of the dogs featured in this book, including Michelle Bariak, Ed Kimble (Mystickal kennels), Maria Novellino and Eva Partida (Tekoneva's Podencos).

IBIZAN HOUND

THE IBIZAN HOUND IN HISTORY

With its early ancestors in ancient Egypt, there is little doubt that the forerunners of today's Ibizan Hound are the same Middle Eastern dogs that lie behind the Pharaoh Hound. The breed's origins date back at least 5,000 years, and these beginnings were often depicted in early Egyptian art, on papyrus, rocks and stones, as well as on tombs and pyramids. It is even said that bone discovery from the Proto-Dynastic Period date such dogs to 4770 BCE.

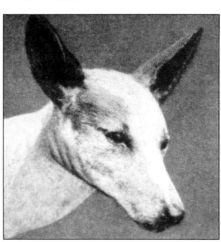

The history of the Ibizan Hound goes back thousands of years to ancient Egypt. This Ibizan Hound is from the 1930s.

Going back still further, prehistoric drawings that are around 8,000 years old, and appear on the walls of the Tassili caves at Hoggar in Algeria, depict primitive spear-bearing hunters with hounds. The hounds in these illustrations appear to be trained and are pursuing and possibly entrapping mountain sheep. The hounds are lean, agile and, what's more, prick-eared!

A particularly interesting find is the Golenischeff plate, a concave dish dating back to around 3100 BCE, found at a site called Nagada. This plate shows us three leashed hounds, all with erect ears and tall, lean bodies, so they are undoubtedly similar to today's Ibizan Hounds. Similar drawings have also been located in the tombs of Hemaku (3100 BCE) and of Ptolomy and Nefermat (2650 BCE), as well as the tombs of Mereku and the famous Tutankhamen (1327 BCE).

In Egyptian mythology, Anubis, also called Anpu, was the inventor of embalming and was the guardian of tombs. He was also the judge of the dead. In appearance he was likened to the dog and was equally watchful, both by day and by night. We can easily see why breed enthusiasts connect Anubis with the Ibizan Hound, as his full life-sized statue found in Tutankhamen's tomb is often said to be "the identical duplicate of the Ibizan Hound today." To be fair, though, there is still controversy among Egyptologists as to whether Anubis was a dog or a jackal, which he was originally thought to be.

In ancient Egypt, there is evidence that dogs of this general type were used to hunt hare, gazelle, antelope and ibex. It is also fascinating to note that in Egypt, not only humans but also dogs were mummified, and mummies of dogs measuring 22 inches (56 cm) at the shoulder have been discovered. Such mummification ensured that they could enter the afterlife.

THE IBIZAN HOUND IN THE BALEARIC ISLES

The Phoenicians, who came from the Arabian Peninsula around 1200 BCE, established great cities at Beirut, Byblos, Tyre, Sidon and Baalbek, expanding across not only North Africa but also western Europe. They pushed past the Straits of Gibraltar and founded the city of Gades (now Cadiz) in Spain.

PODENCO, PODENGO—LET'S CALL THE WHOLE THING OFF!

The Spanish say "Podenco" and the Portuguese say "Podengo," and both refer to similar hare-hunting sighthound dogs from the peninsula. The three breeds of Podengos Portuguêses (translated as Portuguese Rabbit Hounds) include the Pequeño, Medio and Grande (Small, Medium and Large), ranging in size from 22 to 28 inches for the Grande, 15 to 22 inches for the Medio and 8 to 12 inches for the Pequeño. Each breed can be seen in a rough, long or smooth coat, and the coloration ranges from a soft honey to a deep chestnut with or without white markings.

The Spanish breeds include the Podenco Ibicenco, the subject of this book, and the Podenco Andaluz, which like the Portuguese Podengos come in three sizes and three coat types. The Andalusian breed derives from Cadiz and appears similar to the Egyptian hounds. The third Podenco breed is the Podenco Canario, developed on the Canary Islands; it is similar to the Ibizan Hound, but has only a smooth coat and is a few inches shorter.

CHOOSY MATERS

When the Ibizan Hounds were taken to the Balearic Islands, it is said that some of them even refused to mate with other canines. This is not so strange as it may seem, as to this day there are undoubtedly Ibizans who are very choosy about their mates!

In the eighth and ninth centuries BCE, the Phoenicians took their hounds on trading ships to the Balearic Islands off the Spanish mainland. It was one of these islands, Ibiza, that gave the breed its name, and in Spain the dog we know as the Ibizan Hound is called the Podenco Ibicenco or Ca Eivissenc in Catalonia.

There is a fascinating story that might just be true. It tells of Ibizan Hounds riding atop Hannibal's elephants when he invaded Italy. When we consider that Hannibal (247–182 BCE), the Carthaginian general and leader of the famous march across the Alps, was actually born in Ibiza and is said to have traveled with his hounds, there may indeed be some element of truth in this.

In Ibiza and in the neighboring island of Formentora, Ibizan Hounds have

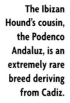

The Ibizan Hound's cousin, the Podenco Andaluz, is an extremely rare breed deriving from Cadiz.

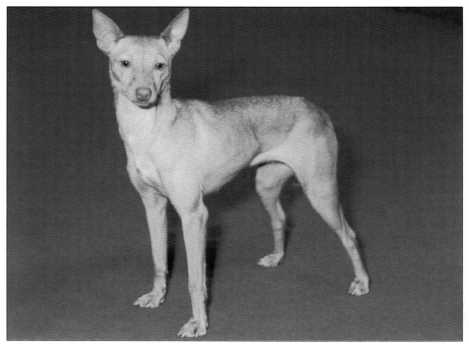

long been known. Here they were bred as "rabbit dogs," for use without guns. The farmers kept only those dogs that were the keenest and strongest hunters, for to earn their keep they had to help feed the farmer's family, as food was scarce. The majority of males and all the weakest puppies were drowned in the sea; those that survived had to be survivors in the truest sense. Their diet was usually a few fish heads and a little goat meat, in addition to what little game they could obtain themselves.

The Ibizan is a sighthound that hunts primarily by vision, although scent and hearing are also used. The Ibizan's huge ears can almost be described as antennae. All sighthounds are adept at following fast, agile prey, and there are many aspects of their construction that help them in this, such as their long legs and elongated middle toes that help with firm footing.

Although the Ibizan Hound was initially worked primarily with rabbit, it has been known to bring down much larger game, including deer. This is a particularly fast and intelligent hound that can hunt on all types of terrain and can follow its quarry in and out of brush. Even walls do not deter these magnificent hunters. If an Ibizan should lose sight of its quarry in heavy cover, it simply stands on

its hind legs to relocate the game. Essentially the Ibizan locates its prey by scent, flush and chase. When the prey is caught, the Ibizan breaks its neck, and this remarkable hound then puts its retrieving skills to work. It is truly a superb, superior hunter!

In Spain usually eight to ten hounds are hunted together, generally all bitches or one male

This speedy and agile sighthound was once a highly decorated hunter.

with several bitches; to avoid quarrels among the males, only one male dog is hunted at a time. They interact well together and encircle the prey, thereby preventing escape. The majority of hunts with Ibizan Hounds end in success. To see an Ibizan hunting is a remarkable sight, for their jumps often incorporate a turn in the air. Jumping up to great heights allows them to survey the scene even in the 4-feet high grasses.

Here are three different-sized Portuguese Warren Hounds, relatives of the Ibizan, that were exhibited at the 2001 World Dog Show in Oporto, Portugal.

The Ibizan Hound is now found throughout the Balearic Islands and also on the mainland of Spain. It was mostly the Ibizan's hunting expertise that kept the breed alive until the middle of the 20th century, when Dona Maria Dolores Olives de Cotonera, the Marquesa de Belgida, became involved with this remarkable breed. She had a breeding kennel on the Balearic Island of Majorca and promoted the breed throughout Spain and beyond.

THE BREED AS A HUNTER IN FRANCE

Because of its silent style of hunting, the Ibizan Hound and similar crosses were used by southern French poachers. These dogs were called Charnegue, or Charnigue, and according to Count Henry Bylandt's work *Hunderassen,* published in 1904 in various languages including English, the weight of the Charnegue, which he also called the Balearic Greyhound, was about 66 pounds, and it measured about 25.5 inches at the shoulder.

VIEWS ON THE BREED IN THE EARLY 20TH CENTURY

Robert Leighton's *The New Book of the Dog* was published in 1907 and was one of very few books of its time that gave coverage to many of the less well-known breeds. In his section titled "French and Other Continental Hounds," he refers to a Podengo "peculiar to the Balearic Isles, although one may occasionally see it in the neighborhood of Valencia, Barcelona and other places along the eastern shores of Spain, where it is known as the Charnigue."

Unfortunately Leighton seems not to have been suitably impressed by this extraordinarily talented hound and, to this author's eyes, elegant breed, for he describes it as lean, ungainly, with a long muzzle, long erect ears and stilty legs. Says Leighton, "it gives one the impression that it is masquerading as a Greyhound or an overgrown Whippet." Mercifully he shows a little more kindness to the breed when he talks of its innate sporting qualities and says that "with training it might be made a creditable hound."

THE IBIZAN HOUND ARRIVES IN BRITAIN

It was in the 1920s that the first Ibizan Hounds arrived in Britain, but it is thought that these died of distemper. Four further imports came into the country in 1929, of which two, Petra of Chardia and Anita of Chardia, were shown at the famous Crufts dog show. But it

A Podengo Portuguêse at a Moscow show.

was not until much later that imports were bred from, and it is to these hounds of the 1960s that the lineage of today's UK stock can be traced. Sol and Curra are particularly notable. Then, in the mid-1970s, Ra Benji Hassan was imported. Although there have been several imports over the decades, the gene pool has generally remained small in the UK, where the breed has never been numerically strong.

The English Ibizan Hound Club was officially approved by

Ch. King Tut's Nefertiti, one of the top winners soon after AKC breed recognition, shown winning the Hound Group at the Kennel Club of Pasadena in 1982, owner handled by Manette Ward under judge Lorraine Masley.

The Kennel Club on September 27, 1965, with an impressive list of founder members. Diana Berry was the club's first secretary, and later she became its president. The first show was held on April 8, 1972. It was for hunting dogs of ancient Egypt, scheduling classes for Ibizan Hounds, Pharaoh Hounds, Basenjis and Sloughis. The club received championship status in 1984, and at its first such show drew an entry of 43 hounds, with an overall entry of 100. Today, at championship shows in the UK numbers exhibited are significantly fewer; large all-breed shows like Crufts and the West of England Ladies Kennel Society attract only a couple dozen hounds.

THE IBIZAN HOUND IN THE US
The Ibizan Hound was initially introduced to the US in 1956 by Colonel and Mrs. Consuelo Seoane, who lived in Rhode Island. The Seoanes imported Hannibal (Stop) and Certera (Tanit) who produced the first litter of eight puppies, four of each sex. These dogs along with several other imports became the country's foundation stock.

The flyer from the litter was Malchus V, a typey male puppy who was sold to Mr. and Mrs. Free lee Preu, Mr. Free lee Preu then being the Ambassador to Spain. Also in 1956, the Seoanes established a parent club for the breed, the Ibizan Hound Club of America (IHCA), for which the Colonel was president for the first eight years. Upon his death in 1964, his wife, Rhoda Low Seoane, resumed the office.

Barcelona's Dona Maria Dolores Olives de Cotonera was glad that interest had been generated in the US, and personally saw to it that quality specimens were sent over to use in early breeding programs.

By the mid-1960s, the breed's popularity was strong enough to petition the American Kennel Club for Miscellaneous Class status. It's reported that there were 151 Ibizan Hounds in the US in 1965. Miscellaneous Class status was granted in 1968. A second club was formed in 1972 by a splinter group of former IHCA members; it was named the Ibizan Hound Fanciers and Exhibitors of the United States. The club only last about four years and was disbanded in favor of the original club.

Best of Breed at Westminster in 2000, Ch. Hemato's J-Mark Star Maiden, handled by Pam Lambie under judge Gloria Reese.

American breeders trying to expand the limited gene pool in the US looked to English breeders. These imports from England proved more reliable than certain Spanish imports that were bred during the mid-1970s. Although there were pivotal breeders like Dolores Olives de Cotonera, stock from other Spanish sources proved disappointing and did not produce the consistent quality that American show breeders sought.

The Ibizan Hound fancy in the US owes a great debt to Richard Edwards of the Ishtar prefix. Edwards promoted the breed with his outstanding English import Int. Ch. Eridu Maestro of Loki, known to all as "Maya," who became the foundation sire of the breed in the US. As the top Ibizan Hound from 1974 through 1977, Maya was the first member of his breed to win the Kennel Review Top Producer award, which he won in 1979. Pedigree buffs are awed by Maya's influence on American Ibizans, citing his presence in every pedigree of the first 100 champions of the breed. Other noteworthy Ishtar Ibizans include Tallaway's Castanet of Loki, Bushland Issa of Curtis Lane, Int. Ch. Ishtar Alpha Ra-de Koo Kay and Ibia of Loki. The Ishtar hounds became the foundation of other kennels as well. Some examples include: Ch. Ishtar Sonnet of Loki, owned by Susan Stafford; Ch. Ishtar Threehand Aquilla of O'Bre-on's, owned by Kathleen O'Brien; and Ch. Ishtar Charisma, owned by Lisa Puskas and Dale Whitmore.

It wasn't until 1979 that the Ibizan Hound was recognized as an American Kennel Club (AKC) breed, making its first appearance at the well-known Westminster Kennel Club Dog Show in 1980.

In 1992 the Ibizan Hound Club of the United States became the AKC parent club for the Ibizan Hound. The club encourages and promotes quality in the breeding of purebred Ibizan Hounds and is in favor of the organization of independent local Ibizan Hound specialty clubs in those locations where there are sufficient fanciers of the breed to meet the requirements of the AKC.

Although today there are many Ibizan Hounds who have placed and won Groups and even Bests in Show, we would be remiss without talking about the top-winning Ibizan Hound in US history: "Bunny," formally known as Ch. Luxor's Playmate of the Year. Owned by Wendy Marquardt, Leslie Lucas, Glen Brand and Dr. Helen

Goldberg, Bunny was the first Ibizan to win the Group at Westminster and was the top Ibizan from 2000 through 2003, winning multiple all-breed and specialty Bests in Show. She became an exquisite ambassador for the breed and converted many to become avid fans of this beautiful sighthound breed.

AROUND THE WORLD

The Ibizan Hound is now known in many different countries around the world, where it is kept not only as a show dog and as a pet but also for use on race tracks and in hunting and coursing competitions. Remarkably, in 1958, a special commission from the Egyptian government was sent to the islands of Ibiza and Formentora to see the breed and, as a result, imported some Ibizans back to their homeland.

The Ibizan Hound has been known in Canada since 1981. Among the breeders responsible for the breed's development and maintenance are Mary Jane Weir of the Titian kennels, Beverly Tufford of the Amar kennels and Mariette Murphy of the Atakah kennels. The breed is active in conformation as well as lure coursing. The first Ibizan to win a Best in Show in Canada was Am/Can/Ber. Ch. Atakah's Flying Cub, owned by Mariette Murphy. The first imports to Australia went there from the UK; lines therefore went back to imports the UK acquired from Ibiza. The first Ibizan Hound litter in Australia was whelped in 1985.

IBIZANS AND LURE COURSING

Because of the breed's history and purpose in life as a hunter, the Ibizan excels at lure coursing. The breed has instinctively retained its natural coursing ability and is still sometimes referred to as "the three-way hunter" because it uses sight, sound and scent. In the US, Ibizans are highly competitive in the American Sighthound Field Association (ASFA) field trials, which involve chasing an artificial lure.

IBIZAN HOUND

The Ibizan Hound has stunningly beautiful, clean-cut lines, and with its light pigmentation and large, erect ears it undoubtedly has a unique appearance. But appearance is not everything. Would-be owners must realize that the Ibizan is a hunting hound and its instinct is still strong. This means that it is not a breed to be taken on lightly and is not usually considered a breed for an urban dweller or city slicker. It needs a lot of exercise, and because of its desire to chase prey it should only be allowed to run free in an absolutely safe, enclosed area, unless it has been fully trained in obedience, so that it comes instantly when called. However, sighthounds rarely come when called and almost never instantly.

The Ibizan Hound is also noted for its ability as a great escape artist and can jump remarkable heights of over 6 feet from a standstill. Many Ibizans are also expert diggers and a good number of them are adept at opening door handles, so beware. Keep in mind, too, that Ibizan Hounds are capable of sprinting at full speed for great distances.

The Ibizan Hound always has his eye out for prey and will require a properly fenced yard to serve as his "hunting grounds."

PERSONALITY
An intelligent breed, the Ibizan Hound is both dignified and independent. This is a breed that is reserved with strangers so is considered rather aloof, but it is perfectly devoted to its owners. The breed is rather sensitive and does not take kindly to harsh scolding. You will certainly see this in your hound's expression, and you will probably regret having chastised him. It goes without saying that no dog should ever be punished physically; raising your voice in reprimand is usually enough to prevent future wrongdoing, excessive barking or other unwanted behaviors.

This is a breed that is slow to mature and high puppy-like activity levels can continue up to the age of around three years. The Ibizan is constructed such that he can reach almost anything in sight, so high counters and tabletops can never be considered out of range.

The Ibizan is not a nervous or aggressive breed, but it truly relishes any opportunity to chase anything that moves. Like most other sighthound breeds, it rarely barks while chasing or hunting.

Some people do keep their Ibizan Hounds in an outdoor environment, but this is only possible in a temperate climate, and warm bedding is absolutely essential. The majority of owners feel this breed is neither physically nor temperamentally suited to outdoor living, so many keep the Ibizan as a house pet. It certainly seems to enjoy home life, frequently taking advantage of the most comfortable armchair or sofa. Ibizan Hounds like to be an integral part of family life, and in return they will give both love and devotion to their dedicated owners.

Although not a protective guard dog, the ever-alert Ibizan can be a good watchdog that is likely to bark loudly at the approach of strangers. It is not recommended, however, to train your dog to be a watchdog. Indeed they may even vocally advise

HEART-HEALTHY
In this modern age of ever-improving cardio-care, no doctor or scientist can dispute the advantages of owning a dog to lower a person's risk of heart disease. Studies have proven that petting a dog, walking a dog and grooming a dog all show positive results toward lowering your blood pressure. The simple routine of exercising your dog—going outside with the dog and walking, jogging or playing catch—is heart-healthy in and of itself. If you are normally less active than your physician thinks you should be, adopting a dog may be a smart option to improve your own quality of life as well as that of another creature.

their owners of a passing bird. However, some Ibizans seem to be much quieter than others, so a dog's own personality comes into play in this regard. It is always important to allow an Ibizan Hound to have plenty of interesting things to occupy its time, including the companionship of humans, other dogs and plenty of interactive toys. A hound left alone for long periods of time will find its own way of keeping busy and can do considerable damage!

IBIZANS WITH CHILDREN AND OTHER PETS
Introductions to children must be made under careful supervision for the Ibizan is a pack animal and considers any human, be it adult or child, a member of his pack. It is important that the

hound understands that his owner is the ultimate pack leader.

Ideally an Ibizan Hound should have been introduced to children and other pets by the age of about 8 to 12 weeks. If initial introductions are made later than this they will be more difficult, but once an Ibizan has come to understand and accept children and other pets he will usually get on well with them. Naturally, owners must teach dogs and children to respect each other from the very first introduction, and young children with dogs should always be kept under close supervision.

It should also be considered that although Ibizan Hounds can

An Ibizan Hound will get along with children as long as they learn how to properly interact with one another.

get along well with their own family's pets, if not restrained, they will almost certainly chase any neighborhood cats, as well as rabbits or indeed anything than runs, hops, flies or jumps!

PHYSICAL CHARACTERISTICS

The Ibizan Hound is a tall, narrow and finely built hound and an agile, tireless and controlled hunter. Not just a hunter though, the Ibizan will also retrieve to hand.

The forelegs are long and straight, the pasterns of good length and the feet have well-arched toes, thick pads and light-colored nails. In this breed the front feet may turn slightly outward. Unlike most other breeds, the Ibizan should have quite a distance between the bottom of the rib cage and the elbow. Hindquarters are long, strong, straight and lean. There are to be no hind dewclaws.

The skull is long, fine and flat and the occipital bone is prominent. Between the eyes the

stop is not well defined, and the muzzle is very slightly convex. The length of the muzzle, from nose to eyes, is the same as the distance from eyes to occiput.

The flesh-colored nose, which tends to harmonize with the coat color, protrudes beyond the teeth, which are perfectly even and white, the upper teeth closely overlapping the lower ones in a scissors bite. Teeth should be set square to the strong jaws, and the thin lips are without dewlap.

The expressive eyes are clear amber, almond-like in shape and neither prominent nor round. The AKC breed standard describes the eye color as clear amber to caramel. The eye rims may be fully or partially pigmented.

The Ibizan Hound has very characteristic ears which are large, thin, stiff and highly mobile. When the dog is alert, the ears are

Generally, the Ibizan Hound will get along with other household pets, but introductions must be properly supervised.

A SENSITIVE HOUND

Ibizan Hounds, like Pharaoh Hounds, can blush; indeed they are highly sensitive and expressive canines. They are not, however, a suitable breed for everyone, and potential owners should do their homework thoroughly before deciding that the Ibizan Hound is really the breed for them.

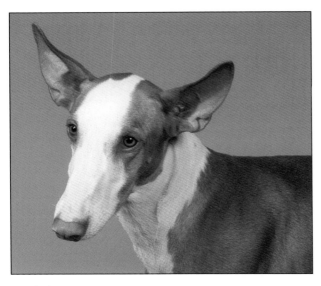

The Ibizan is a sensitive dog that won't respond well to harsh treatment. Who could be unkind to such an adorable face?

should never be curled within itself or low over the back. The AKC standard describes the tail as being carried in a sickle, ring or saber position, according to the mood and the individual dog.

In the breed's homeland, size varies considerably, from between 22 and 29 inches, but balance is the overriding factor. In the US, the breed standard's height guidance is 22.5 to 26 inches at withers, but it also gives guidance as to weight; 50 pounds for dogs and 45 for bitches. The AKC standard states that the Ibizan Hound is slightly longer than it is tall. This is a breed with strong, flat muscling, with no sign of heaviness.

The Ibizan Hound has a long, far-reaching stride, with a slight hover before placing the foot to the ground, effectively a suspended trot.

There are two coat types, smooth or rough. It is always hard, dense and close, and longer under the tail and at the back of the legs. Both types of coat are untrimmed.

The longer of the two coats, the wire-haired, can be from 1 to 3 inches in length and may occasionally have a generous mustache.

The Ibizan Hound's color must always be white, chestnut or lion, either as a solid color or in any combination. The AKC standard says simply white or

erect, in a continuous line with the arch of the neck when viewed in profile. The base of the ear is set on level with the eyes. This highly mobile ear can point forward, sideways or even fold backward according to the dog's mood. However, it should never droop, bend or crease.

The tail is long, thin and low set, reaching well below the hock; when passed around the flank, it reaches the spine. When excited the tail may be carried high but

HOUND BUSINESS
Ibizan Hounds can be willful and they do tend to get bored easily. It is always important that they have plenty of suitably sturdy toys with which to play, and of course regular human companionship is an absolute must.

red, but the red can range from light through a yellowish red (called lion) to deep red, again either solid or in any combination.

THE ALLURE OF COURSING

Ibizan Hounds are good at lure coursing, following the lure for the simple joy of giving chase. Watching an Ibizan Hound fly around a course, you will become immediately aware of the breed's tremendous athleticism. Lure coursing is a fun and exciting way to fake a real hunt, though this does not give the hound the opportunity to turn and manipulate, as would be the case when chasing live prey.

WARMING UP AND DOWN

If participating in lure coursing it is sensible to allow Ibizan Hounds to warm up and get stretched out before they have an opportunity to sprint at full speed. Afterwards, if they are walked a while, they have a chance to cool down, preventing stiffness. They should be encourage to drink lots of water for rehydration and to urinate to shed lactic acid.

HEALTH CONSIDERATIONS

The Ibizan Hound is generally a healthy breed, and the number of hereditary problems that has been found in Ibizans is relatively small compared to

many other breeds. Ibizan Hounds, like other sighthounds, do not tolerate some anesthetics well, so this should certainly be mentioned to your veterinarian prior to an operation being performed. There are anesthetics that are suitable for the Ibizan, and your vet should be familiar with them.

The following section of this chapter pinpoints a few problems in the breed and other more general problems one should be aware of so that any encountered can be dealt with as early as possible.

DEAFNESS

Occasionally Ibizan Hounds have been found to be deaf in one or both ears. Puppies of all breeds are born blind and deaf. Their ear

As owner it will be your responsibility to make sure that your Ibizan Hound remains in good health so that your relationship remains a long and happy one.

canals are closed and normally begin to open between 12 and 16 days of age. However, with deaf puppies a group of nerve cells in the ear that detect sound begin to deteriorate, a process that is usually complete by the time the pup is six weeks old and is irreversible.

Testing by BAER (Brainstem Auditory Evoked Response) is quick and easy and can be performed on very young puppies without anesthesia. Although sires and dams can also be tested, this should not be taken as an assurance that the puppies will not suffer from the disorder.

Beware of the insecticides you use in your yard, as they may have an ill effect on your Ibizan Hound.

SEIZURES

Seizures are not unknown in Ibizan Hounds, and the conditions that cause seizures are believed to be hereditary. The causes are many and varied, and unfortunately no testing services are available.

ALLERGIES

Like all breeds, some Ibizan Hounds can be affected by allergies, but others can be totally unaffected. Sometimes it is difficult to ascertain the cause of the allergy. There are many possibilities, ranging from the living-room carpet, shampoo and, quite frequently, certain grasses and molds. In cases of a skin allergy, it is a good idea to change shampoo, conditioning rinse and any other coat sprays used, for these are perhaps the easiest items to eliminate before looking further is necessary.

Food allergies are also not unknown, but once diagnosed these can usually be kept under control with a carefully considered diet. The allergy is often noticed as hot spots on the skin, despite there being no sign of external parasites. A low protein diet often seems to suit skin troubles.

REACTION TO INJECTIONS AND INSECTICIDES

Like other sighthounds, Ibizans can suffer a reaction to modern-

THE AGE OF ROBO-DOG

Studies at the Center for the Human-Animal Bond show that children who interact with pets benefit physiologically, socially and educationally. Dogs, in particular, increase children's learning capacities and expand their abilities to function in social situations. Families with young children commonly add a canine to their homes.

Enter Robo-dog. Efforts to create a robotic canine companion are fast under way, and there have been some interesting results. It is the hope of scientists that the interaction between robotic dogs and children will shed light on the physical, mental, moral and social concepts of such relationships. Robotic dogs offer many advantages over real dogs—they don't require food or water and never have accidents indoors. Even so, Robo-dogs will never take the place of real dogs—even George Jetson's futuristic family included Astro, a real-live dog! It is curious that 21st-century humans would invest so much money and energy into inventing robots to do for us what dogs have been doing for centuries for nothing more than a pat on the head and a bowl of food.

when injections are needed and is especially important in the case of anesthetics. Some Ibizan Hounds can also display sensitivity to insecticides, so this should be taken into account when selecting products for the control of parasites.

AXONAL DYSTROPHY

The Ibizan Hound is believed to have a genetic propensity for axonal dystrophy, a rare neurological problem that affects muscles and movement in young puppies. The disease is being named in consequence of these symptoms being found in a few litters of Ibizans, but there have apparently been no reports in recent years. Experienced breeders will check pedigrees for known carriers before breeding to a dog.

UNDESCENDED TESTICALS

Unilateral cryptorchidism is when one testicle is retained, due usually to a shortening of the cord, thus not allowing the testicle to drop. Unilateral cryptorchidism is often referred to erroneously as monorchidism, but in fact this is different, because the latter is when only one testicle is present. Although dogs that are affected can produce sperm, they should never be used as a stud.

Veterinary advice should be sought regarding whether or not removal of the undescended testicle is advisable.

day injections. The reason for this seems to be that they lack the protective layer of fat under the skin, which the majority of breeds have. This is something that should be discussed with your vet

PATELLA LUXATION

Patella luxation is a substandard formation of the knee joint that affects a number of breeds, though more often the smaller ones. In mild cases there may be no evident signs of the problem, but if more severe, patella luxation can be both painful and disabling, one of the signs being that a leg is lifted intermittently. The hind legs can become bowed and the gait altered, and in the long term arthritis can develop. Occasionally surgery is necessary, and any dog seriously affected should certainly not be bred from.

This agile sighthound will lead an active lifestyle; health tests should be conducted when he's a puppy to assure he's in tip-top shape.

HIP DYSPLASIA

Hip dysplasia is a problem involving the malformation of the ball and socket joint at the hip, a developmental condition caused by the interaction of many genes. This results in looseness of the hip joints and, although not always painful, can cause lameness, and typical movement can be impaired.

Although a dog's environment does not actually cause hip dysplasia, this may have some bearing on how unstable the hip joint eventually becomes. Osteoarthritis can eventually develop as a result of the instability.

Tests for hip dysplasia are available in most countries throughout the world. Both hips are tested and scored individually; the lower the score the less the degree of dysplasia. Clearly dogs with high scores should not be incorporated in breeding programs. In the United States, hip scores are registered with the Orthopedic Foundation for Animals (OFA) or PennHIP.

EYE DISORDERS

There are many eye problems that affect dogs and various different eye tests can be carried out. As testing recommendations and requirements vary from country to country, it is wise to contact an Ibizan Hound breed club to ask about which tests, if any, are expected.

PHOTOGRAPHY BY CAROL BEUCHAT.

The breathtaking beauty of the Ibizan will surely make admirers of anyone this lovely sighthound comes in contact with.

IBIZAN HOUND

INTRODUCTION TO THE BREED STANDARD

A breed standard is essentially a written description of how an ideal specimen of the breed should appear. It is used as a tool by breeders and judges to "standardize" their vision. A breed standard undoubtedly helps breeders to produce stock that comes as close as possible to the recognized standard and helps judges to know exactly what they are looking for. This enables judges to make a carefully considered decision when selecting the most typical Ibizan Hound present to head their line of winners.

Each kennel club has a different breed standard for each of its breeds. The breed standard for the Ibizan Hound was originally drafted by the Ibizan Hound Club of the United States, the breed's official AKC parent club. The standard is then adopted by the AKC. In England, the breed standard is set down by The Kennel Club, which controls all of its standards.

Although some breed standards are more comprehensive than others, all are designed effectively to paint a picture in words. However, each reader will almost certainly have a slightly different way of interpreting these words. After all, when all is said and done, were everyone to interpret a breed's standard in exactly the same way, there would only be one consistent winner within the breed at any given time.

That said, from the standard certain things are made clear. For

Head study of a smooth-coated Ibizan in profile showing correct type, structure and proportion.

example, the Ibizan standard tells us the color of the eye, the pigmentation, the fact that the ears are large, thin, stiff and highly mobile. So we can see at a glance that a so-called Ibizan with a very dark eye, black pigment and a heavy dropped ear would be completely uncharacteristic.

The breed standards drawn up in the UK and in the US do, however, vary in some respects. Among other things, there is discrepancy regarding shoulders and layback for the former requires rather steep, short shoulder blades, while the AKC standard calls for the shoulders to be well laid back, but joined to a rather upright upper arm. Thus one can see that breeds can be developed to vary somewhat from country to country.

In any event, to fully comprehend the intricacies of a breed, reading words alone is never enough. It is essential for devotees to watch other Ibizan Hounds being judged at shows and, if possible, to attend seminars at which the breed is discussed. This enables owners to absorb as much as possible about this highly individual breed. Hands-on experience, providing an opportunity to assess the structure of dogs, is always valuable, especially for those who hope ultimately to judge the breed.

First we present the official breed standard of the AKC,

A smooth-coated Ibizan in profile showing correct type, structure and proportion.

followed by the English standard of The Kennel Club.

AKC STANDARD FOR THE IBIZAN HOUND

General Appearance: The Ibizan's clean-cut lines, large prick ears and light pigment give it a unique appearance. A hunting dog whose quarry is primarily rabbits, this ancient hound was bred for thousands of years with function being of prime importance. Lithe and racy, the Ibizan possesses a deer-like elegance combined with the power of a hunter. Strong, without appearing heavily muscled, the Ibizan is a hound of moderation. With the exception of the ears, he should not appear extreme or exaggerated.

The Ibizan Hound's head should be finely chiseled, revealing an elegant expression.

Head study of a wirehaired Ibizan showing full face with characteristic large upright ears.

In the field the Ibizan is as fast as top coursing breeds and without equal in agility, high jumping and broad jumping ability. He is able to spring to great heights from a standstill.

Size, Proportion, Substance: *Size*—The height of dogs is 23.5 inches to 27.5 inches at the withers. Bitches are 22.5 to 26 inches at the withers. There is no preference for size within this range. Sizes slightly over or under the norms are not to be regarded as demerits when other qualities are good. *Weight*—Average weight of dogs is 50 pounds; bitches, 45 pounds. *Proportion*—Slightly longer than tall. *Substance*—The Ibizan possesses clean, fine bone. The muscling is strong, yet flat, with no sign of heaviness.

Head: Long and narrow in the form of a sharp cone truncated at its base. Finely chiseled and extremely dry fleshed.

Expression: The Ibizan has an elegant, deer-like look. The eyes are oblique and small, ranging in color from clear amber to caramel. The rims are the color of the nose and are fully or partially pigmented. The appearance of the eye is intelligent, alert and inquisitive. The ears are large, pointed and natural. On alert the ear should never droop, bend or crease. Highly mobile, the ear can point forward, sideways or be folded backward, according to mood. On alert, the lowest point of the base is at level of the eye. On frontal examination, the height of the ear is approximately 2.5 times that of the widest point of the base.

Skull: Long and flat, prominent occipital bone, little defined stop; narrow brow. The muzzle is elongated, fine and slender with a very slight Roman convex. The length from the eyes to point of nose is equal to the distance from eyes to occiput. The muzzle and skull are on parallel planes. The nose is prominent, extending beyond the lower jaw. It is of a rosy flesh color, never black or liver, and tends to harmonize with that of the coat. Pigment is solid or butterfly. Nostrils are open. Lips are thin and tight and the color of the nose. Flews are tight and dry fleshed. *Bite*—The teeth are perfectly opposed in a scissors bite; strong and well set.

Neck, Topline, Body: The neck is long, slender, slightly arched and strong, yet flat muscled. The topline, from ears to tail, is

A wire-haired Ibizan in profile showing correct type, structure and proportion.

smooth and flowing. The back is level and straight. *Body*—The chest is deep and long with the breastbone sharply angled and prominent. The ribs are slightly sprung. The brisket is approximately 2.5 inches above the elbow. The deepest part of the chest, behind the elbow, is nearly to or to the elbow. The abdomen is well tucked up, but not exaggerated. The loin is very slightly arched, of medium breadth and well muscled. The croup is very slightly sloping.

The wire-haired Ibizan is allowed a generous mustache, although it is not always prominent.

FAULTS IN PROFILE

Ewe-necked, upright shoulders, shallow chest, narrow front and toes out, flat feet, lacking angulation behind.

Generally coarse and lacking elegance, heavy head, short neck, weak pasterns, long back, soft topline, high in the rear, ring tail, cow-hocked.

chest. It is well held in but not so much as to restrict movement. *Legs*—The forearms are very long, strong, straight and close, lying flat on the chest and continuing in a straight line to the ground. Bone is clean and fine. The pasterns are strong and flexible, slightly sloping, with well developed tendons. Dewclaw removal is optional. *Feet*—Hare-foot. The toes are long, closed and very strong. Interdigital spaces are well protected by hair. Pads are durable. Nails are white.

Hindquarters: Angulation is moderate with the hindquarters being set under the body. *Legs*—The thighs are very strong with flat muscling. The hocks are straight when viewed from the rear. Bone is clean and fine. There are no rear dewclaws. The feet are as in front.

Coat: There are two types of coat; both untrimmed. *Short*—Shortest on head and ears and longest at back of *the* thighs and under the tail. Wire-haired can be from 1 to 3 inches in length with a possible generous moustache. There is more hair on the back, back of thighs, and tail. Both types of coat are hard in texture and neither coat is preferable to the other.

Color: White or red, (from light, yellowish-red called "lion" to deep red), solid or in any

The tail is set low, highly mobile, and reaches at least to the hock. It is carried in a sickle, ring or saber position, according to the mood and individual specimen.

Forequarters: Angulation is moderate. The shoulders are elastic but never loose with moderate breadth at the withers. The shoulder blades are well laid back. At the point of the shoulder they join to a rather upright upper arm. The elbow is positioned in front of the deepest part of the combination. No color or pattern is preferable to the other. Disqualify any color other than white or red.

Gait: An efficient, light and graceful single tracking movement. A suspended trot with joint flexion when viewed from the side. The Ibizan exhibits smooth reach in front with balanced rear drive, giving the appearance of skimming over the ground.

Temperament: The Ibizan Hound is even-tempered, affectionate and loyal. Extremely versatile and trainable, he makes an excellent family pet, and is well suited to the breed ring, obedience, tracking and lure-coursing. He exhibits a keen, natural hunting instinct with much determination and stamina in the field.

Disqualification: Any color other than white or red.

Approved September 11, 1989
Effective November 1, 1989

THE KENNEL CLUB STANDARD FOR THE IBIZAN HOUND

General Appearance: Tall, narrow, finely built, large erect ears.

Characteristics: Agile, tireless, controlled hunter. Retrieves to hand, has ability to jump great heights without take-off run.

While red and white are the only acceptable colors according to the breed standard, there is no preferable patterning.

Temperament: Reserved with strangers, not nervous or aggressive. Dignified, intelligent and independent.

Head and Skull: Fine, long, flat skull with prominent occipital bone. Stop not well defined, slightly convex muzzle, length of which from eyes to tip of nose equals length from eyes to occiput. Nose flesh coloured, should protrude beyond teeth, jaws very strong and lean.

Eyes: Clear amber, expressive. Almond-shaped; not prominent, large or round.

Ears: Large, thin, stiff, highly mobile, erect when dog is alert, in a continuous line with arch of neck when viewed in profile; base set on level with eyes. Drop ears unacceptable.

Mouth: Perfectly even white teeth; scissors bite, i.e. upper teeth closely overlapping lower teeth and set square to the jaws. Thin lips with no dewlap.

Neck: Very lean, long, muscular and slightly arched.

Forequarters: Rather steep, short shoulder blades, long straight legs, erect pasterns of good length.

Body: Level back sloping slightly from the pin bones to rump. Long, flat ribcage. Short coupled with

While there are many similarities between the AKC standard and England's Kennel Club standard, there is allowance in Britain for hunting scars without penalty.

well tucked-up waist, breast bone very prominent. Depth measured between bottom of ribcage and elbow 7–8 cms (2.5–3 ins).

Hindquarters: Long, strong, straight and lean, no great angulation, long second thigh, turning neither in nor out.

Feet: Well arched toes, thick pads, light coloured claws. Front feet may turn slightly outwards. Dewclaws should not be removed in front. No hind dewclaws.

Tail: Long, thin, low set, reaching well below the hock; when passed between legs and round flank reaches spine; may be carried high when excited, but not curled within itself or low over back.

Gait/Movement: A suspended trot, which is a long far-reaching stride, with a slight hover before placing foot to ground.

Coat: Smooth or rough always hard, close, dense. Longer under tail and at back of legs. Hunting scars should not be penalised.

Colour: White, chestnut or lion solid colour, or any combination of these.

Size: In country of origin varies between 56 and 74 cms (22–29 ins), but balance is overriding factor.

Faults: Any departure from the foregoing points should be considered a fault and the seriousness with which the fault should be regarded should be in exact proportion to its degree and its effect upon the health and welfare of the dog.

Note: Male animals should have two apparently normal testicles fully descended into the scrotum.

March 1994

BREEDING FOR DOLLARS!

Are you thinking about breeding your bitch so that you can make a quick, easy profit by selling the puppies? Why not! You know that raising a litter is no work at all—the dogs take care of themselves! Stop right there. Before you start building that whelping box, let reality be your roadblock.

There is no money in breeding dogs. Consider the costs involved: the bitch's maintenance and special care; the food, formula and veterinary bills for the dam and her pups; the equipment needed to convert part of your home into a kennel, etc. Once you've paid for these things (and there's more!), you wouldn't break even were you to get top dollar for every puppy, which you won't! If you're looking to make money, get a real estate license, become a professional caterer, sell your kid's toys or grandmother's china on eBay®— something along those lines. Any of those ventures will prove more profitable, and then you'll have more money to spend on your canine best friend.

IBIZAN HOUND

HOW TO SELECT A PUPPY

Before beginning your search for an Ibizan Hound puppy, make absolutely sure that this is the right dog for you, your family and your living situation. Don't be swayed by the puppy photographs in this book. All puppies of every breed are cute and irresistible, and so are mixed breed and mongrel puppies. What makes you certain the Ibizan is the breed for you?

There is no disputing the fact that the Ibizan Hound is a very

You will know a breeder is trustworthy if you notice a happy relationship between her and her dogs.

special breed, but the pros and cons must be carefully weighed against each other before reaching the important decision that this dog is going to enter your life. The Ibizan Hound is an active, demanding dog; he is not a small dog; his hunting instincts are still very much intact; and he is a sensitive, intelligent and challenging canine who deserves the right home. Consider also that the breed is numerically small and only a handful of litters are produced in the US, UK and other countries. Are you certain that one of these precious puppies belongs in your care?

When you have made that decision, you must also ask yourself why you want an Ibizan, whether purely as a pet, as a show dog or for lure coursing. Perhaps you have a large piece of property and a disparaging pack of rabbits or hares terrorizing your garden or hobby farm.

The number of breeders in your area is likely quite small, so you should plan to travel to meet the breeder in person. Rely upon the parent club's website to locate responsible breeders. The club's breeder referral service provides names, phone numbers and addresses. Make an effort to phone the breeder to discuss the availability of a puppy. Tell the breeder exactly why you want an Ibizan Hound when you make your initial inquiries, for you will almost certainly need to take the breeder's advice as to which available puppy displays the most promise for the show ring, lure coursing or rabbit hunting. If looking for a pet, you should have discussed your family situation with the breeder and, again, taken advice as to which puppy is likely to suit you best.

After you find a suitable breeder, make plans to visit the kennel and meet the litter. Watch the puppies interact together and see which little personality appeals to you most, obviously taking into account the overall quality of the dog, especially if destined for a show home. Don't expect an Ibizan puppy to be the perfect example of balance and symmetry. It will take some time for a puppy to feel comfortable in his own paws, and his legs are growing faster than his whiskers though his ears are definitely keeping up. A young Ibizan puppy, ironically, resembles a jack rabbit, his very quarry! By the way, it's not advised to take home a puppy that is overly shy, as such a dog may encounter problems in socializing. If you

COST OF OWNERSHIP
The purchase price of your puppy is merely the first expense in the typical dog budget. Quality dog food, veterinary care (sickness and health maintenance), dog supplies and grooming costs will add up to big bucks every year. Can you adequately afford to support a canine addition to the family?

suspect a puppy is shyer than the others, ask the breeder for his opinion. Perhaps she's not shy, she's smart. It's possible that the females in the litter are more laid back and low key (a wise way to keep out of the path of their wild brothers). Alternatively, the breeder may tell you that the puppy you think is shy and retiring was just playing with mom while the others were sleeping. Don't write off a puppy because he's sleepy or smart enough not to compete with his pawing, mauling siblings.

You should have done plenty of background homework on the breed, preferably have visited a dog show or two and have met a few nice dogs and their breeders. If you're serious about Ibizans and are thinking about showing or competing, search out a national or regional specialty show where you can see the breed in relatively large numbers. This will afford you the option of seeing great

With such adorable puppies, your decision can be difficult. Be sure to take your breeder's recommendation into account when making your choice.

dogs with their breeders and owners and help you determine which lines you like the best.

Remember that the dog you select should remain with you for the duration of his life, which is usually between 12 and 14 years, so making the right decision from the outset is of utmost importance. No dog should be moved from one home to another simply because his owners were careless, hasty or impulsive. It is always important to remember that when looking for a puppy, a good breeder will be assessing you as a prospective new owner just a carefully as you are selecting the breeder. As we've said, all puppies are captivating and tempting, but you must select a healthy, well-bred puppy from a caring breeder who has given the litter the attention they deserve and has looked after them well. It is important for breeders to

socialize puppies as early as possible, and it should be apparent when you meet the puppies. Although Ibizan Hounds are discriminating and loyal as adults, the puppies should be friendly and cavalier with their kisses and affection. A properly socialized litter will crawl over one another to get the closest to a new visitor. When you encounter a happy, demonstrative litter like this, you know the breeder has done his job.

The puppy you select should look well fed, but not pot-bellied, as this might indicate worms. Eyes should look bright and clear, without discharge. The nose should be moist, an indication of good health, but should never be runny, and it goes without saying

TEMPERAMENT ABOVE ALL ELSE

Regardless of breed, a puppy's disposition is perhaps his most important quality. It is, after all, what makes a puppy lovable and "livable." If the puppy's parents or grandparents are known to be snappy or aggressive, the puppy is likely to inherit those tendencies. That can lead to serious problems, such as the dog's becoming a biter, which can lead to eventual abandonment.

that there should certainly be no evidence of loose movements, nor of parasites. The puppy you choose should also have a healthy looking coat, an important indicator to good health internally. Look carefully at the puppies' teeth, ears, eyes and nails. These attributes complete the portrait of good health.

Of course, the Ibizan Hound puppy you select should look like an Ibizan. Ask the breeder to explain the breed standard to you if there are points that you're not completely sure of. Most importantly, however, is the health of the puppy. The AKC parent club, the Ibizan Hound Club of the United States (IHCUS) requires that breeders test for at least two of the following hereditary conditions: hips, elbow, eyes, axonal dystrophy, thyroid and hearing. The IHCUS Code of Ethics requires that all breeding stock is tested. Ask to see the documentation of the sire and dam when you visit the kennel. If the breeder hasn't bothered testing, you are wise to seek out another breeder.

Ask the breeder for permission to meet other dogs on the property, in addition to the dam and sire. Sometimes the sire is not available because he lives with another breeder. This is very common and no cause for alarm. The dam, however, must be on the property, especially if the puppies

SIGNS OF A HEALTHY PUPPY
Healthy puppies are robust little fellows who are alert and active, sporting shiny coats and supple skin. They should not appear lethargic, bloated or pot-bellied, nor should they have flaky skin or runny or crusted eyes or noses. Their stool should be firm and well formed, with no evidence of blood or mucus.

are eight weeks old or younger. The condition of the adults speaks volumes about the breeder's care and maintenance of the dogs. A breeder who knows all of the special qualities of each dog he introduces you to is a breeder who loves his dogs. If the dogs are affectionate and familiar with the breeder, you can feel confident that he really spends time with the dogs and doesn't regard them merely as breeding stock or competition animals.

The decision to live with a Ibizan Hound is a serious commitment and not one to be taken lightly. This puppy is a living sentient being that will be dependent on you for basic survival for his entire life. Beyond the basics of survival—food, water, shelter and protection—he needs much, much more. The new pup needs love, nurturing and a proper canine education to mold him into a responsible, well-behaved canine citizen. Your Ibizan Hound's health and good manners will need consistent monitoring and regular "tune-ups," so your job as a responsible dog owner will be ongoing throughout every stage of his life. If you are not prepared to accept these responsibilities and commit to them for the next decade, likely longer, then you are not prepared to own a dog of any breed.

Although the responsibilities of owning a dog may at times tax your patience, the joy of living with your Ibizan Hound far outweighs the workload, and a well-mannered adult dog is worth your time and effort. Before your very eyes, your new charge will grow up to be your most loyal friend, devoted to you unconditionally.

Your Ibizan Hound puppy will be looking to you to provide him with the love and care he needs. Are you up to the challenge?

YOUR IBIZAN HOUND SHOPPING LIST

Just as expectant parents prepare a nursery for their baby, so should you ready your home for the arrival of your Ibizan Hound pup. If you have the necessary puppy supplies purchased and in place before he comes home, it will ease the puppy's transition from the warmth and familiarity of his mom and littermates to the brand-new environment of his new home and human family. You will be too busy to stock up and prepare your house after your pup comes home, that's for sure! Imagine how a pup must feel upon being transported to a strange new place. It's up to you to comfort him and to let your little pup know that he is going to be happy with you.

FOOD AND WATER BOWLS

Your puppy will need separate bowls for his food and water. Stainless steel pans are generally preferred over plastic bowls since they sterilize better and pups are less inclined to chew on the metal. Heavy-duty ceramic bowls

When you find a conscientious, knowledgeable breeder, you will know it by the quality of the puppies.

are popular, but consider how often you will have to pick up those heavy bowls! Buy adult-sized pans, as your puppy will grow into them before you know it.

THE DOG CRATE

If you think that crates are tools of punishment and confinement for when a dog has misbehaved, think again. Most breeders and almost all trainers recommend a

Stainless steel food and water bowls are the best for your pup, as they are less inclined to chew on them.

crate as the preferred house-training aid as well as for all-around puppy training and safety. Because dogs are natural den creatures that prefer cave-like environments, the benefits of crate use are many. The crate provides the puppy with his very own "safe house," a cozy place to sleep, take a break or seek comfort with a favorite toy; a travel aid to house your dog when on the road, at motels or at the vet's office; a training aid to help teach your puppy proper toileting habits; and a place of solitude when non-dog people happen to drop by and don't want a lively puppy—or even a well-behaved adult dog—saying hello or begging for attention.

Crates come in several types, although the wire crate and the fiberglass airline-type crate are the

Your local pet-supply shop will have plenty of crates to choose from. Pictured are the fiberglass (TOP), wire (BOTTOM RIGHT) and mesh (BOTTOM LEFT) crates.

> ## SAFE HAVEN
> Many owners of Ibizan Hounds find a large crate to be of invaluable assistance. Of course dogs should only be confined to a crate for short periods of time, but most come to look upon it as a safe place and enjoy being there, provided they have been trained to accept this from a young age. A crate can be useful when you need to confine your hound for some reason, such as if you have visitors to the home who are not particularly dog-friendly.

most popular. Both are safe and your puppy will adjust to either one, so the choice is up to you. The wire crates offer better visibility for the pup as well as better ventilation. Many of the wire crates easily collapse into suitcase-size carriers. The fiberglass crates, similar to those used by the airlines for animal transport, are sturdier and more den-like. However, the fiberglass crates do not collapse and are less ventilated than a wire crate, which can be problematic in hot weather. Some of the newer crates are made of heavy plastic mesh; they are very lightweight and fold up into slim-line suitcases. However, a mesh crate might not be suitable for a pup with manic chewing habits.

Don't bother with a puppy-sized crate. Although your Ibizan

Hound will be a wee fellow when you bring him home, he will grow up in the blink of an eye and your puppy crate will be useless. Purchase a crate that will accommodate an adult Ibizan Hound. He will stand about 27 inches when full grown, so a medium- to large-sized crate will fit him nicely.

BEDDING AND CRATE PADS

Your puppy will enjoy some type of soft bedding in his "room" (the crate), something he can snuggle into to feel cozy and secure. Old towels or blankets are good choices for a young pup, since he may (and probably will) have a toileting accident or two in the crate or decide to chew on the bedding material. Once he is fully trained and out of the early chewing stage, you can replace the puppy bedding with a permanent crate pad if you prefer. Crate pads and other dog beds run the gamut from inexpensive to high-end doggie-designer styles, but don't splurge on the good stuff until you are sure that your puppy is reliable and won't tear it up or make a mess on it.

PUPPY TOYS

Just as infants and older children require objects to stimulate their minds and bodies, puppies need toys to entertain their curious brains, wiggly paws and achy teeth. A fun array of safe doggie

It is better to provide your pup with a crate pad instead of lining his "den" with newspaper.

toys will help satisfy your puppy's chewing instincts and distract him from gnawing on the leg of your antique chair or your new leather sofa. Most puppy toys are cute and look as if they would be a lot of fun, but not all are necessarily safe or good for your puppy, so use caution when you go puppy-toy shopping.

Although Ibizan Hounds are not known to be voracious chewers like many other dogs, they still love to chew. The best "chewcifiers" are nylon and hard rubber bones, which are safe to gnaw on and come in sizes appropriate for all age groups and breeds. Be especially careful of natural bones, which can splinter or develop dangerous sharp edges; pups can easily swallow or choke on those bone splinters. Veterinarians often tell of surgical nightmares involving bits of splintered bone, because in

TOYS 'R SAFE

The vast array of tantalizing puppy toys is staggering. Stroll through any pet shop or pet-supply outlet and you will see that the choices can be overwhelming. However, not all dog toys are safe or sensible. Most very young puppies enjoy soft woolly toys that they can snuggle with and carry around. (You know they have outgrown them when they shred them up!) Avoid toys that have buttons, tabs or other enhancements that can be chewed off and swallowed. Soft toys that squeak are fun, but make sure your puppy does not disembowel the toy and remove (and swallow) the squeaker. Toys that rattle or make noise can excite a puppy, but they present the same danger as the squeaky kind and so require supervision. Hard rubber toys that bounce can also entertain a pup, but make sure that the toy is too big for your pup to swallow.

addition to the danger of choking, the sharp pieces can damage the intestinal tract.

Similarly, rawhide chews, while a favorite of most dogs and puppies, can be equally dangerous. Pieces of rawhide are easily swallowed after they get all gummy from chewing, and dogs have been known to choke on large pieces of ingested rawhide. Rawhide chews should be offered only when you can supervise the puppy.

Soft woolly toys are special puppy favorites. They come in a wide variety of cute shapes and sizes; some look like little stuffed animals. Puppies love to shake them up and toss them about or simply carry them around. Be careful of fuzzy toys that have button eyes or noses that your pup could chew off and swallow, and make sure that he does not disembowel a squeaky toy to remove the squeaker. Braided rope toys are similar in that they are fun to chew and toss around, but they shred easily and the strings are easy to swallow. The strings are not digestible and, if the puppy doesn't pass them in his stool, he could end up at the vet's office. As with rawhides, your puppy should be closely monitored with rope toys.

If you believe that your pup has ingested one of these forbidden objects, check his stools for the next couple of days to see

A word of caution about homemade toys: be careful with your choices of non-traditional play objects. Never use old shoes or socks, since a puppy cannot distinguish between the old ones on which he's allowed to chew and the new ones in your closet that are strictly off limits. That principle applies to anything that resembles something that you don't want your puppy to chew.

COLLARS

A lightweight nylon collar is the best choice for a very young pup. Quick-click collars are easy to put on and remove, and they can be adjusted as the puppy grows. Introduce him to his collar as soon as he comes home to get him accustomed to wearing it. He'll get used to it quickly and won't mind a bit. Make sure that it is snug enough that it won't slip off, yet

When outdoors, provide your curious Ibizan pup with safe chew toys to keep him from finding something dangerous to "play" with.

Select a collar that is lightweight, adjustable and comfortable for the dog.

if he passes them when he defecates. At the same time, also watch for signs of intestinal distress. A call to your veterinarian might be in order to get his advice and be on the safe side.

An all-time favorite toy for puppies (young and old!) is the empty gallon milk jug. Hard plastic juice containers—46 ounces or more—are also excellent. Such containers make lots of noise when they are batted about, and puppies go crazy with delight as they play with them. However, they don't often last very long, so be sure to remove and replace them when they get chewed up on the ends.

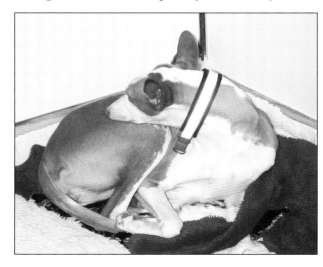

loose enough to be comfortable for the pup. You should be able to slip two fingers between the collar and his neck. Check the collar often, as puppies grow in spurts, and his collar can become too tight almost overnight. Choke collars are for training purposes only and should never be used on a puppy under five months old.

LEASHES

A 6-foot nylon lead is an excellent choice for a young puppy. It is lightweight and not as tempting to chew as a leather lead. You can switch to a 6-foot leather lead after your pup has grown and is used to walking politely on a lead. For initial puppy walks and house-training purposes, you should invest in a shorter lead so that you have more control over the puppy. At first, you don't

want him wandering too far away from you, and when taking him out for toileting you will want to keep him in the specific area chosen for his potty spot.

Once the puppy is heel trained with a traditional leash, you can consider purchasing a retractable lead. A retractable lead is excellent for walking adult dogs that are already leash-wise. This type of lead allows the dog to roam farther away from you and explore a wider area when out walking, and also retracts when you need to keep him close to you.

HOME SAFETY FOR YOUR PUPPY

The importance of puppy-proofing cannot be overstated. In addition to making your house comfortable for your Ibizan Hound's arrival, you also must make sure that your house is safe for your puppy before you bring him home. There are countless hazards in the owner's personal living environment that a pup can sniff, chew, swallow or destroy. Many are obvious;

The puppy may view his leash as a chew toy, so you must be consistent in training and in redirecting his chewing.

COLLARING OUR CANINES

The standard flat collar with a buckle or a snap, in leather, nylon or cotton, is widely regarded as the everyday all-purpose collar. If the collar fits correctly, you should be able to fit two fingers between the collar and the dog's neck.

Leather Buckle Collars

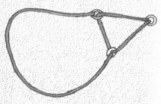

Limited-Slip Collar

Snap-Bolt Choke Collar

The martingale, Greyhound or limited-slip collar is preferred by many dog owners and trainers. It is fixed with an extra loop that tightens when pressure is applied to the leash. The martingale collar gets tighter but does not "choke" the dog. The limited-slip collar should only be used for walking and training, not for free play or interaction with another dog. These types of collar should never be left on the dog, as the extra loop can lead to accidents.

Choke collars, usually made of stainless steel, are made for training purposes but are not recommended for small dogs or heavily coated breeds. The chains can injure small dogs or damage long/abundant coats. Thin nylon choke leads are commonly used on show dogs while in the ring, though they are not practical for everyday use.

The harness, with two or three straps that attach over the dog's shoulders and around his torso, is a humane and safe alternative to the conventional collar. By and large, a well-made harness is virtually escape-proof. Harnesses are available in nylon and mesh and can be outfitted on most dogs ranging in chest girths of 10 to 30 inches.

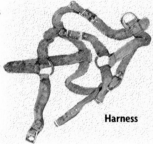

Harness

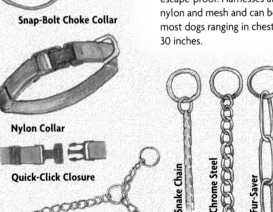

Nylon Collar

Quick-Click Closure

Snake Chain

Chrome Steel

Fur-Saver

Choke Chain Collars

A head collar, composed of a nylon strap that goes around the dog's muzzle and a second strap that wraps around his neck, offers the owner better control over his dog. This device is recommended for problem-solving with dogs (including jumping up, pulling and aggressive behaviors) but must be used with care.

A training halter, including a flat collar and two straps, made of nylon and webbing, is designed for walking. There are several on the market; some are more difficult to put on the dog than others. The halter harness, with two small slip rings at each end, is recommended for ease of use.

Leash Life

Dogs love leashes! Believe it or not, most dogs dance for joy every time their owners pick up their leashes. The leash means that the dog is going for a walk—and there are few things more exciting than that! Here are some of the kinds of leashes that are commercially available.

Nylon Leash

Leather Leash

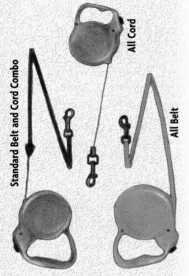

Standard Belt and Cord Combo

All Cord

All Belt

Retractable Leashes

Traditional Leash: Made of cotton, nylon or leather, these leashes are usually about 6 feet in length. A quality-made leather leash is softer on the hands than a nylon one. Durable woven cotton is a popular option. Lengths can vary up to about 48 feet, designed for different uses.

Chain Leash: Usually a metal chain leash with a plastic handle. This is not the best choice for most breeds, as it is heavier than other leashes and difficult to manage.

Retractable Leash: A long nylon cord is housed in a plastic device for extending and retracting. This leash, also known as a flexible leash, is ideal for taking trained dogs for long walks in open areas, although it is not always suitable for large, powerful breeds. Different lengths and sizes are available, so check that you purchase one appropriate for your dog's weight.

Elastic Leash: A nylon leash with an elastic extension. This is useful for well-trained dogs, especially in conjunction with a head halter.

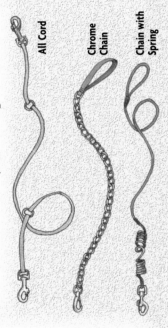

All Cord

Chrome Chain

Chain with Spring

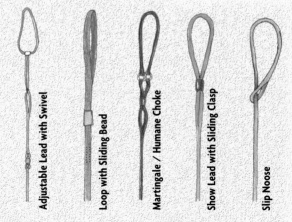

Adjustable Lead with Swivel

Loop with Sliding Bead

Martingale / Humane Choke

Show Lead with Sliding Clasp

Slip Noose

A Variety of Collar-Leash-in-One Products

Avoid leashes that are completely elastic, as they afford minimal control to the handler.

Adjustable Leash: This has two snaps, one on each end, and several metal rings. It is handy if you need to tether your dog temporarily, but is never to be used with a choke collar.

Tab Leash: A short leash (4 to 6 inches long) that attaches to your dog's collar. This device serves like a handle, in case you have to grab your dog while he's exercising off lead. It's ideal for "half-trained" dogs or dogs that listen only half of the time.

Slip Leash: Essentially a leash with a collar built in, similar to what a dog-show handler uses to show a dog. This British-style collar has a ring on the end so that you can form a slip collar. Useful if you have to catch your own runaway dog or a stray.

A DOG-SAFE HOME

The dog-safety police are taking you on a house tour. Let's go room by room and see how safe your own home is for your new pup. The following items are doggy dangers, so either they must be removed or the dog should be monitored or not allowed access to these areas.

LIVING ROOM
- house plants (some varieties are poisonous)
- fireplace or wood-burning stove
- paint on the walls (lead-based paint is toxic)
- lead drapery weights (toxic lead)
- lamps and electrical cords
- carpet cleaners or deodorizers

OUTDOORS
- swimming pool
- pesticides
- toxic plants
- lawn fertilizers

BATHROOM
- blue water in the toilet bowl
- medicine cabinet (filled with potentially deadly bottles)
- soap bars, bleach, drain cleaners, etc.
- tampons

KITCHEN
- household cleaners in the kitchen cabinets
- glass jars and canisters
- sharp objects (like kitchen knives, scissors and forks)
- garbage can (with remnants of good-smelling things like onions, potato skins, apple or pear cores, peach pits, coffee beans and other harmful tidbits)
- food left out on counters (some foods are toxic to dogs)

GARAGE
- antifreeze
- fertilizers (including rose foods)
- pesticides and rodenticides
- pool supplies (chlorine and other chemicals)
- oil and gasoline in containers
- sharp objects, electrical cords and power tools

There is plenty going on outdoors that will attract your Ibizan's attention. The only way to assure your hound's safety when outdoors is to keep him on leash.

Scout your home for tiny objects that might be seen at a pup's eye level. Keep medication bottles and cleaning supplies well out of reach, and do the same with waste baskets and other trash containers. It goes without saying that you should not use rodent poison or other toxic chemicals in any puppy area and that you must keep such containers safely locked up. You will be amazed at how many places a curious puppy can discover!

Once your house has cleared inspection, check your yard. A sturdy fence, well embedded into the ground, will give your dog a safe place to play and potty. Ibizan Hounds are second to none when it comes to jumping ability, so a fence at least 6-feet high is necessary to contain an agile youngster or adult. Check the fence periodically for necessary repairs. If there is a weak link or space to squeeze through, you can be sure a determined Ibizan Hound will discover it.

others are not. Do a thorough advance house check to remove or rearrange those things that could hurt your puppy, keeping any potentially dangerous items out of areas to which he will have access.

Electrical cords are especially dangerous, since puppies view them as irresistible chew toys. Unplug and remove all exposed cords or fasten them beneath baseboards where the puppy cannot reach them. Veterinarians and firefighters can tell you horror stories about electrical burns and house fires that resulted from puppy-chewed electrical cords. Consider this a most serious precaution for your puppy and the rest of your family.

The garage and shed can be hazardous places for a pup, as things like fertilizers, chemicals and tools are usually kept there. It's best to keep these areas off limits to the pup. Antifreeze is especially dangerous to dogs, as they find the taste appealing and it takes only a few licks from the driveway to kill a dog, puppy or adult, small breed or large.

VISITING THE VETERINARIAN

A good veterinarian is your Ibizan Hound puppy's best health-insurance policy. If you do not already have a vet, ask friends and experienced dog people in your area for recommendations so that you can select a vet before you bring your Ibizan Hound puppy home. Also arrange for your puppy's first veterinary examination beforehand, since many vets have two- and three-week waiting periods and your puppy should visit the vet within a day or so of coming home.

It's important to make sure your puppy's first visit to the vet is a pleasant and positive one. The vet should take great care to befriend

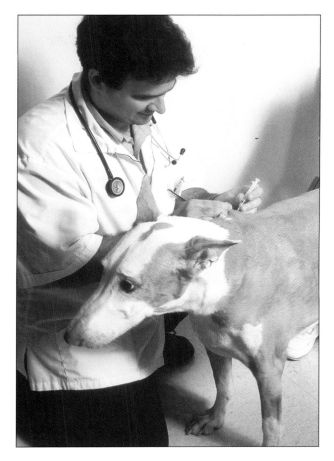

the pup and handle him gently to make their first meeting a positive experience. The vet will give the pup a thorough physical examination and set up a schedule for vaccinations and other necessary wellness visits. Be sure to show your vet any health and inoculation records, which you should have received from your breeder. Your vet is a great source of canine health information, so be sure to

Your vet will start your Ibizan Hound's vaccination program when the dog is young and will manage his booster inoculations throughout the dog's life.

Puppies are investigative and must be kept confined safely to keep them out of danger and mischief.

ask questions and take notes. Creating a health journal for your puppy will make a handy reference for his wellness and any future health problems that may arise.

MEETING THE FAMILY

Your Ibizan Hound's homecoming is an exciting time for all members of the family, and it's only natural that everyone will be eager to meet him, pet him and play with him. However, for the puppy's sake, it's best to make these initial family meetings as uneventful as possible so that the pup is not overwhelmed with too much too soon. Remember, he has just left his dam and his littermates and is away from the breeder's home for the first time. Despite his fuzzy wagging tail, he is still apprehensive and wondering where he is and who all these strange humans are. It's best to let him explore on his own and meet the family members as he feels comfortable. Let him investigate all the new smells, sights and sounds at his own pace. Children should be especially careful to not get overly excited, use loud voices or hug the pup too tightly. Be calm, gentle and affectionate, and be ready to comfort him if he appears frightened or uneasy.

Be sure to show your puppy his new crate during this first day home. Toss a treat or two inside the crate; if he associates the crate with food, he will associate the crate with good things. If he is comfortable with the crate, you can offer him his first meal inside it. Leave the door ajar so he can wander in and out as he chooses.

FIRST NIGHT IN HIS NEW HOME

So much has happened in your Ibizan Hound puppy's first day away from the breeder. He's had his first car ride to his new home. He's met his new human family and perhaps the other family pets.

He has explored his new house and yard, at least those places where he is to be allowed during his first weeks at home. He may have visited his new veterinarian. He has eaten his first meal or two away from his dam and litter-mates. Surely that's enough to tire out an eight-week-old Ibizan Hound pup—or so you hope!

It's bedtime. During the day, the pup investigated his crate, which is his new den and sleeping space, so it is not entirely strange to him. Line the crate with a soft towel or blanket that he can snuggle into and gently place him into the crate for the night. Some breeders send home a piece of bedding from where the pup slept with his littermates, and those familiar scents are a great comfort for the puppy on his first night without his siblings.

He will probably whine or cry. The puppy is objecting to the confinement and the fact that he

CONFINEMENT

It is wise to keep your puppy confined to a small "puppy-proofed" area of the house for his first few weeks at home. Gate or block off a space near the door he will use for outdoor potty trips. Expandable baby gates are useful to create puppy's designated area. If he is allowed to roam through the entire house or even only several rooms, it will be more difficult to house-train him.

is alone for the first time. This can be a stressful time for you as well as for the pup. It's important that you remain strong and don't let the puppy out of his crate to comfort him. He will fall asleep eventually. If you release him, the puppy will learn that crying means "out" and will continue that habit. You are laying the groundwork for future habits. Some breeders find that soft music can soothe a crying pup and help him get to sleep.

SOCIALIZING YOUR PUPPY

The first 20 weeks of your Ibizan Hound puppy's life are the most important of his entire lifetime. A properly socialized puppy will grow up to be a confident and stable adult who will be a pleasure to live with and a welcome addition to the neighborhood.

The importance of socialization cannot be overemphasized. Research on canine behavior has proven that puppies who are not exposed to new sights, sounds, people and animals during their first 20 weeks of life will grow up to be timid and fearful, even aggressive, and unable to flourish outside of their home environment.

Socializing your puppy is not difficult and, in fact, will be a fun time for you both. Lead training goes hand in hand with socialization, so your puppy will be learning how to walk on a lead at the same time that he's meeting the neighborhood. Because the Ibizan Hound is a such a unique breed, everyone will enjoy meeting "the new kid on the block." Take him for short walks to the park and to other dog-friendly places where he will encounter new people, especially children. Puppies automatically recognize children as "little people" and are drawn to play with them. Just make sure that you supervise these meetings and that the children do not get too rough or encourage him to play too hard. An overzealous pup can often nip too hard, frightening the child and in turn making the puppy overly excited. A bad experience in puppyhood can impact a dog for life, so a pup that has a negative experience with a child may grow up to be shy or even aggressive around children.

Take your puppy along on your daily errands. Puppies are natural "people magnets," and most people who see your pup will want to pet him. All of these encounters will help to mold him into a confident adult dog. Likewise, you will soon feel like a confident, responsible dog owner, rightly proud of your handsome Ibizan Hound.

Be especially careful of your puppy's encounters and experiences during the eight-to-ten-week-old period, which is also called the "fear period." This is a serious imprinting period, and all contact during this time should be gentle and positive. A frightening or negative event could leave a permanent impression that could affect his future behavior if a similar situation arises.

Also make sure that your puppy has received his first and second rounds of vaccinations before you expose him to other dogs or bring him to places that other dogs may frequent. Avoid dog parks and other strange-dog areas until your vet assures you that your puppy is fully immunized and resistant to the diseases that can be passed between canines. Discuss socialization with your breeder, as some breeders recommend socializing the puppy even before he has

---

THE CRITICAL SOCIALIZATION PERIOD

Canine research has shown that a puppy's 8th through 16th week is the most critical learning period of his life. This is when the puppy "learns to learn," a time when he needs positive experiences to build confidence and stability. Puppies who are not exposed to different people and situations outside the home during this period can grow up to be fearful and sometimes aggressive. This is also the best time for puppy lessons, since he has not yet acquired any bad habits that could undermine his ability to learn.

It is through interaction with littermates that a puppy will learn many valuable life lessons.

received all of his inoculations, depending on how outgoing the puppy may be.

LEADER OF THE PUPPY'S PACK
Like other canines, your puppy needs an authority figure, someone he can look up to and regard as the leader of his "pack." His first pack leader was his dam, who taught him to be polite and not chew too hard on her ears or nip at her muzzle. He learned those same lessons from his litter-mates. If he played too rough, they cried in pain and stopped the game, which sent an important message to the rowdy puppy.

As puppies play together, they are also struggling to determine who will be the boss. Being pack animals, dogs need someone to be in charge. If a litter of puppies remained together beyond puppyhood, one of the pups would emerge as the strongest one, the one who calls the shots.

Once your puppy leaves the pack, he will look intuitively for a new leader. If he does not recognize you as that leader, he will try to assume that position for himself. Of course, it is hard to imagine your adorable Ibizan Hound puppy trying to be in charge when he is so small and

It is normal behavior for puppies to use their mouths to get to know one another. This shouldn't be mistaken for aggression.

seemingly helpless. You must remember that these are natural canine instincts. Do not cave in and allow your pup to get the upper "paw"!

Just as socialization is so important during these first 20 weeks, so too is your puppy's early education. He was born without any bad habits. He does not know what is good or bad behavior. If he does things like nipping and digging, it's because he is having fun and doesn't know that humans consider these things as "bad." It's your job to teach him proper puppy manners, and this is the best time to accomplish that—before he has developed bad habits, since it is much more difficult to "unlearn" or correct unacceptable learned behavior

than to teach good behavior from the start.

Make sure that all members of the family understand the

MAKE A COMMITMENT

Dogs are most assuredly man's best friend, but they are also a lot of work. When you add a puppy to your family, you also are adding to your daily responsibilities for years to come. Dogs need more than just food, water and a place to sleep. They also require training (which can be ongoing throughout the lifetime of the dog), activity to keep them physically and mentally fit and hands-on attention every day, plus grooming and healthcare. Your life as you now know it may well disappear! Are you prepared for such drastic changes?

importance of being consistent when training their new puppy. If you tell the puppy to stay off the sofa and your daughter allows him to cuddle on the couch to watch her favorite television show, your pup will be confused about what he is and is not allowed to do. Have a family conference before your pup comes home so that everyone understands the basic principles of puppy training and the rules you have set forth for the pup, and agrees to follow them.

The old saying that "an ounce of prevention is worth a pound of cure" is especially true when it comes to puppies. It is much easier to prevent inappropriate behavior than it is to change it.

It's also easier and less stressful for the pup, since it will keep discipline to a minimum and create a more positive learning environment for him. That, in turn, will also be easier on you.

Here are a few commonsense tips to keep your belongings safe and your puppy out of trouble:

- Keep your closet doors closed and your shoes, socks and other apparel off the floor so your puppy can't get at them.
- Keep a secure lid on the trash container or put the trash where your puppy can't dig into it. He can't damage what he can't reach!
- Supervise your puppy at all times to make sure he is not getting into mischief. If he starts

If you don't want your Ibizan to make himself a permanent fixture of your couch, establish early on in puppyhood that he is not allowed there.

to chew the corner of the rug, you can distract him instantly by tossing a toy for him to fetch. You also will be able to whisk him outside when you notice that he is about to piddle on the carpet. If you can't see your puppy, you can't teach him or correct his behavior.

SOLVING PUPPY PROBLEMS

CHEWING AND NIPPING

Nipping at fingers and toes is normal puppy behavior. Chewing is also the way that puppies investigate their surroundings. However, you will have to teach your puppy that chewing anything other than his toys is not acceptable. That won't happen overnight and at times puppy teeth will test your patience. However, if you allow nipping and chewing to continue, just think about the damage that a mature Ibizan Hound can do with a full set of adult teeth.

Whenever your puppy nips your hand or fingers, cry out "Ouch!" in a loud voice, which should startle your puppy and stop him from nipping, even if only for a moment. Immediately distract him by offering a small treat or an appropriate toy for him to chew instead (which means having chew toys and puppy treats handy or in your pockets at all times). Praise him when he takes the toy and tell him what a good fellow he is. Praise is just as or even more important in puppy training as discipline and correction.

Safe chew toys should be provided to keep your pup's attention away from other appealing "playthings" that could be dangerous.

Puppies also tend to nip at children more often than adults, since they perceive little ones to be more vulnerable and more similar to their litter-mates. Teach your children appropriate responses to nipping behavior. If they are unable to handle it themselves, you may have to intervene. Puppy nips can be quite painful and a child's frightened reaction will only encourage a puppy to nip harder, which is a natural canine response. As with all other puppy situations, interaction between your Ibizan Hound puppy and children should be supervised.

Chewing on objects, not just family members' fingers and ankles, is also normal canine behavior that can be especially tedious (for the owner, not the pup) during the teething period when the puppy's adult teeth are coming in. At this stage, chewing just plain feels good. Furniture legs and cabinet corners are common puppy favorites. Shoes and other personal items also taste pretty good to a pup.

The best solution is, once again, prevention. If you value something, keep it tucked away and out of reach. You can't hide your dining-room table in a closet, but you can try to deflect the chewing by applying a bitter product made just to deter dogs from chewing. Available in a spray or cream, this substance is vile-tasting, although safe for dogs, and most puppies will avoid the forbidden object after one tiny taste. You also can apply the product to your leather

leash if the puppy tries to chew on his lead during leash-training sessions.

Keep a ready supply of safe chews handy to offer your Ibizan Hound as a distraction when he starts to chew on something that's a "no-no." Remember, at this tender age, he does not yet know what is permitted or forbidden, so you have to be "on call" every minute he's awake and on the prowl.

You may lose a treasure or two during puppy's growing-up period, and the furniture could sustain a nasty nick or two. These can be trying times, so be prepared for those inevitable accidents and comfort yourself in knowing that this too shall pass.

Nipping at fingers may be cute when your pup is still a wee little one but won't be so cute when those adult teeth grow in.

The tall Ibizan Hound is certainly a capable jumper, and this behavior should be discouraged while the dog is a puppy.

JUMPING UP

Ibizan Hound pups will grow up to become outstanding jumpers, and will be happy to do so—on you, your guests, your counters and your furniture. This is just another normal part of growing up, and one you need to meet head-on before it becomes an ingrained habit.

The key to jump correction is consistency. You cannot correct your Ibizan Hound for jumping up on you today, then allow it to happen tomorrow by greeting him with hugs and kisses. As you have learned by now, consistency is critical to all puppy lessons.

For starters, try turning your back as soon as the puppy jumps. Jumping up is a means of gaining your attention and, if the pup can't see your face, he may get discouraged and learn that he loses eye contact with his beloved master when he jumps up.

Leash corrections also work, and most puppies respond well to a leash tug if they jump. Grasp the leash close to the puppy's collar and give a quick tug downward, using the command "Off." Do not use the word "Down," since "Down" is used to teach the puppy to lie down, which is a separate action that he will learn during his education in the basic commands. As soon as the puppy has backed off, tell him to sit and immediately praise him for doing so. This will take many repetitions and won't be accomplished quickly, so don't get discouraged or give up; you must be even more persistent than your puppy.

A third method used for jump correction is the spritzer bottle. Fill a spray bottle with water mixed with a bit of lemon juice or vinegar. As soon as puppy jumps, command him "Off" and spritz him with the water mixture. Of course, that means having the spray bottle handy whenever or wherever jumping usually happens.

Yet another method to discourage jumping is grasping the puppy's paws and holding them gently but firmly until he struggles to get away. Wait a brief moment or two, then release his paws and give him a command to sit. He should eventually learn that jumping gets him into an uncomfortable predicament.

Children are major victims of puppy jumping, since puppies view little people as ready targets for jumping up as well as nipping. If your children (or their friends) are unable to dispense jump corrections, you will have to intervene and handle it for them.

Important to prevention is also knowing what you should not do. Never kick your Ibizan Hound (for any reason, not just for jumping) or knock him in the chest with your knee. That maneuver could actually harm your puppy. Vets can tell you stories about puppies who suffered broken bones after being banged about when they jumped up.

PUPPY WHINING

Puppies often cry and whine, just as infants and little children do. It's their way of telling us that they are lonely or in need of attention. Your puppy will miss his littermates and will feel insecure when he is left alone. You may be out of the house or just in another room, but he will still feel alone. During these times, the puppy's crate should be his personal comfort station, a place all his own where he can feel safe and secure. Once he learns that being alone is okay and not something to be feared, he will settle down without crying or objecting. You might want to leave a radio on while he is crated, as the sound of human

HAPPY PUPPIES COME RUNNING

Never call your puppy (or adult dog) to come to you and then scold him or discipline him when he gets there. He will make a natural association between coming to you and being scolded, and he will think he was a bad dog for coming to you. He will then be reluctant to come whenever he is called. Always praise your puppy every time he comes to you. If your dog is behaving in a manner that needs correction, always go to him and deliver your command in a stern voice. This will likely be a sufficient way to stop whatever he shouldn't be doing.

voices can be soothing and will give the impression that people are around.

Give your Ibizan Hound puppy a favorite cuddly toy or chew toy to entertain him whenever he is crated. You will both be happier: the puppy because he is safe in his den and you because he is quiet, safe and not getting into puppy escapades that can wreak havoc in your house or cause him danger.

To make sure that your puppy will always view his crate as a safe and cozy place, never, ever use the crate as punishment. That's the best way to turn the crate into a negative place that the pup will want to avoid. Sure, you can use the crate for your own peace of mind if your puppy is getting into trouble and needs some "time out." Just don't let him know that! Never scold the pup and immediately place him into the crate. Count to ten, give him a couple of hugs and maybe a treat, then scoot him into his crate.

It's also important not to make a big fuss when he is released from the crate. That will make getting out of the crate more appealing to your pup than being in the crate, which is just the opposite of what you are trying to achieve.

It may take some time for your pup to adjust to being confined, but as long as the experiences are kept positive he will soon get used to it.

PROPER CARE OF YOUR

IBIZAN HOUND

Adding an Ibizan Hound to your household means adding a new family member who will need your care each and every day. When your Ibizan Hound pup first comes home, you will start a routine with him so that, as he grows up, your dog will have a daily schedule just as you do. The aspects of your dog's daily care will likewise become regular parts of your day, so you'll both have a new schedule. Dogs learn by consistency and thrive on routine: regular times for meals, exercise, grooming and potty trips are just as important for your dog as they are for you! Your dog's schedule will depend much on your family's daily routine, but remember that you now have a new member of the family who is part of your day every day!

FEEDING

Feeding your dog the best diet is based on various factors, including age, activity level, overall condition and size of breed. When you visit the breeder, he will share with you his advice about the proper diet for your dog based on his experience with the breed and the foods with which he has had success. Likewise, your vet will be a helpful source of advice throughout the dog's life and will aid you in planning a diet for optimal health.

FEEDING THE PUPPY

Of course, your pup's very first food will be his dam's milk. There may be special situations in which pups fail to nurse, necessitating that the breeder hand-feed them with a formula, but for the most part pups spend the first weeks of life nursing from their dam. The

Puppies will be weaned off their mother's milk and introduced to a solid food while still with the breeder.

breeder weans the pups by gradually introducing solid foods and decreasing the milk meals. Pups may even start themselves off on the weaning process, albeit inadvertently, if they snatch bites from their mom's food bowl.

By the time the pups are ready for new homes, they are fully weaned and eating a good puppy food. As a new owner, you may be thinking, "Great! The breeder has taken care of the hard part." Not so fast.

A puppy's first year of life is the time when all or most of his growth and development takes place. This is a delicate time, and diet plays a huge role in proper skeletal and muscular formation. Improper diet and exercise habits can lead to damaging problems that will compromise the dog's health and movement for his entire life. That being said, new owners should not worry needlessly. With the myriad types of food formulated specifically for growing pups of different-sized breeds, dog-food manufacturers have taken much of the guesswork out of feeding your puppy well. Since growth-food formulas are designed to provide the nutrition that a growing puppy needs, it is unnecessary and, in fact, can prove harmful to add supplements to the diet. Research has shown that too much of certain vitamin supplements and minerals predispose a dog to skeletal problems. It's by no means a case of "if a little is good, a lot is better." At every stage of your dog's life, too much or too little in the way of nutrients can be harmful, which is why a manufactured complete food is the easiest way to know that your dog is getting what he needs.

Because of a young pup's small body and accordingly small digestive system, his daily portion will be divided up into small meals throughout the day. This can mean starting off with three or more meals a day and decreasing the number of meals as the pup matures. Eventually you can feed only one meal a day, although it is generally thought that dividing the day's food into two meals on a morning/evening schedule is healthier for the dog's digestion.

Regarding the feeding schedule, feeding the pup at the same times and in the same place each day is important for both housebreaking purposes and establishing the dog's everyday

There continues to be debate on whether feeding from raised bowls is a factor in causing the deadly gastric torsion. Consult your breeder and veterinarian about this pressing issue.

routine. As for the amount to feed, growing puppies generally need proportionately more food per body weight than their adult counterparts, but a pup should never be allowed to gain excess weight. Dogs of all ages should be kept in proper body condition, but extra weight can strain a pup's developing frame, causing skeletal problems.

Watch your pup's weight as he grows and, if the recommended amounts seem to be too much or too little for your pup, consult the vet about appropriate dietary changes. Keep in mind that treats, although small, can quickly add up throughout the day, contributing unnecessary calories. Treats are fine when used prudently; opt for dog treats specially formulated to be healthy or for nutritious snacks like small pieces of cheese or cooked chicken.

FEEDING THE ADULT DOG

For the adult (meaning physically mature) dog, feeding properly is about maintenance, not growth. Again, correct weight is a concern. Your dog should appear fit and should have an evident "waist." His ribs should not be protruding (a sign of being underweight), but they should be covered by only a slight layer of fat. Under normal circumstances, an adult dog can be maintained fairly easily with a high-quality

> ### IBIZAN FEEDING CONSIDERATIONS
> Some owners feed just one meal each day but others feed two, partly because it is considered a precaution against bloat. However frequently you decide to feed your dog, remember that no dog should ever be fed within at least an hour of strenuous exercise. Ideally exercise should be avoided for one hour before and two hours following a meal. Many owners of longer-legged breeds offer food and water in containers that are raised from the ground. While this was thought to aid the passage to the digestive tract, recent studies have proved that the contrary may be true. Feed your dog on the floor, as raised feeding stands may actually increase the likelihood of bloat.
>
> Ibizan puppies thrive best on a diet that consists of 18% fat and 28% protein, never more. Adults should be fed a diet with 10% fat and 21% protein. Higher percentages can lead to allergies, according to some breeders' experiences.

nutritionally complete adult-formula food.

Factor treats into your dog's overall daily caloric intake, and avoid offering table scraps. Overweight dogs are more prone to health problems. Research has even shown that obesity takes years off a dog's life. With that in mind, resist the urge to overfeed and over-treat. Don't make unnecessary additions to your dog's diet, whether with tidbits or with extra vitamins and minerals.

IBIZAN DIET POINTERS

Your Ibizan adolescent, especially the males, may develop a poor appetite. Given the breed's slim conformation, a dog who's a picky eater can look alarmingly thin. While encouraging him to eat is always a good idea, do not lure him toward his bowl with savory, high-fat, high-cal treats or specially prepared roasts and biscuits. The result of your good cooking and intentions will be an Ibizan who's overweight and doesn't like to eat a proper canine diet. A fussy eater is never a blessing.

When feeding an Ibizan Hound, consider what the breed would have eaten centuries ago. Their diet would have comprised fish, rabbit and goat, with wheat grains and a brown rice. Bearing this in mind, some owners feel it unwise to include soy, beef, horse meat, potato or white rice in today's diet.

The amount of food needed for proper maintenance will vary depending on the individual dog's activity level, but you will be able to tell whether the daily portions are keeping him in good shape. With the wide variety of good complete foods available, choosing what to feed is largely a matter of personal preference. Just as with the puppy, the adult dog should have consistency in his mealtimes and feeding place. In addition to a consistent routine, regular mealtimes also allow the owner to see how much his dog is eating. If the dog seems never to be satisfied or, likewise, becomes uninterested in his food, the owner will know right away that something is wrong and can consult the vet.

DIETS FOR THE AGING DOG

A good rule of thumb is that once a dog has reached 75% of his expected lifespan, he has reached "senior citizen" or geriatric status. Your Ibizan Hound will be considered a senior at about 9 years of age; based on his size, he has a projected lifespan of about 12–14 years. (The smallest breeds generally enjoy the longest lives and the largest breeds the shortest.)

What does aging have to do with your dog's diet? No, he won't get a discount at the local diner's early-bird special. Yes, he will require some dietary changes to accommodate the changes that come along with increased age. One change is that the older dog's dietary needs become more similar to that of a puppy. Specifically, dogs can metabolize more protein as youngsters and seniors than in the adult-mainte-nance stage. Discuss with your vet whether you need to switch to a higher-protein or senior-formulated food or whether your current adult-dog food contains sufficient nutrition for the senior.

Watching the dog's weight remains essential, even more so in the senior stage. Older dogs are already more vulnerable to illness, and obesity only contributes to their susceptibility to problems. As the older dog becomes less active and, thus, exercises less, his regular portions may cause him to gain weight. At this point, you may consider decreasing his daily food intake or switching to a reduced-calorie food. As with other changes, you should consult your vet for advice.

TYPES OF FOOD AND
READING THE LABEL
When selecting the type of food to feed your dog, it is important to check out the label for ingredi-ents. Many dry-food products have soybean, corn or rice as the main ingredient. The main ingredient will be listed first on the label, with the rest of the ingredients following in descending order according to

their proportion in the food. While these types of dry food are fine, you should also look into dry foods based on meat or fish. These are better-quality foods and thus higher priced. However, they may be just as economical in the long run, because studies have shown that it takes less of the higher-quality foods to maintain a dog.

Comparing the various types of food, dry, canned and semi-moist, dry foods contain the least amount of water and canned foods the most. Proportionately, dry foods are the most calorie- and nutrient-dense, which means that you need more of a canned food product to supply the same amount of nutrition. In households domiciling breeds of disparate size, the canned/dry/semi-moist question can be of special importance. Larger breeds obviously eat more than smaller ones and thus in

HOLD THE ONIONS
Sliced, chopped, grated; dehydrated, boiled, fried or raw; pearl, Spanish, white or red: onions can be deadly to your dog. The toxic effects of onions in dogs are cumulative for up to 30 days. A serious form of anemia, called Heinz body anemia, affects the red blood cells of dogs that have eaten onions. For safety (and better breath), dogs should avoid chives and scallions as well.

general do better on dry foods, but smaller breeds do fine on canned foods and require "small bite" formulations to protect their small mouths and teeth if fed only dry foods. So if you have breeds of different size in your household, consider both your own preferences and what your dogs like to eat, but in the main think canned for the little guys and dry or semi-moist for everyone else. You may find success mixing the food types

While every dog, young or old, loves a treat, it is important not to over-treat your Ibizan Hound, as he will get all the nutrition he needs from his food.

> ## QUENCHING HIS THIRST
>
> Is your dog drinking more than normal and trying to lap up everything in sight? Excessive drinking has many different causes. Obvious causes for a dog's being thirstier than usual are hot weather and vigorous exercise. However, if your dog is drinking more for no apparent reason, you could have cause for concern. Serious conditions like kidney or liver disease, diabetes and various types of hormonal problems can all be indicated by excessive drinking. If you notice your dog's being excessively thirsty, contact your vet at once. Hopefully there will be a simpler explanation, but the earlier a serious problem is detected, the sooner it can be treated, with a better rate of cure.

as well. Water is important for all dogs, but even more so for those fed dry foods, as there is no high water content in their food.

There are strict controls that regulate the nutritional content of dog food, and a food has to meet the minimum requirements in order to be considered "complete and balanced." It is important that you choose such a food for your dog, so check the label to be sure that your chosen food meets the requirements. If not, look for a food that clearly states on the label that it is formulated to be complete and balanced for your dog's particular stage of life.

Recommendations for amounts to feed will also be indicated on the label. You should also ask your vet about proper food portions, and you will keep an eye on your dog's condition to see whether the recommended amounts are adequate. If he becomes over- or underweight, you will need to make adjustments; this also would be a good time to consult your vet.

The food label may also make feeding suggestions, such as whether moistening a dry-food product is recommended. Sometimes a splash of water will make the food more palatable for the dog and even enhance the flavor. Don't be overwhelmed by the many factors that go into feeding your dog. Manufacturers of complete and balanced foods make it easy, and once you find the right food and amounts for your Ibizan Hound, his daily feeding will be a matter of routine.

DON'T FORGET THE WATER!
For a dog, it's always time for a drink! Regardless of what type of food he eats, there's no doubt that he needs plenty of water. Fresh cold water, in a clean bowl, should be freely available to your dog at all times. There are special circumstances, such as during puppy housebreaking, when you will want to monitor your pup's water intake so that you will be able to predict when he will need

to relieve himself, but water must be available to him nonetheless. Water is essential for hydration and proper body function just as it is in humans.

You will get to know how much your dog typically drinks in a day. Of course, in the heat or if exercising vigorously, he will be more thirsty and will drink more. However, if he begins to drink noticeably more water for no apparent reason, this could signal any of various problems, and you are advised to consult your vet.

Water is the best drink for dogs. Some owners are tempted to give milk from time to time or to moisten dry food with milk, but dogs do not have the enzymes necessary to digest the lactose in milk, which is much different from the milk that nursing puppies receive. Therefore stick with clean fresh water to quench your dog's thirst, and always have it readily available to him.

It is important that your Ibizan Hound has water available to him indoors and outdoors, especially in warmer climates.

Photography by Carol Beuchat.

opportunity to run free so as to stretch his limbs as well as to release pent-up energy.

Free runs should, of course, only be allowed in places that are

When let off leash to exercise, which should be in a secure area with adequate fencing, your Ibizan Hound should always wear his collar and proper identification tags.

A word of caution concerning your deep-chested dog's water intake: he should never be allowed to gulp water, especially at mealtimes. In fact, his water intake should be limited at mealtimes as a rule. This simple daily precaution can go a long way in protecting your dog from the dangerous and potentially fatal gastric torsion (bloat).

EXERCISE

The Ibizan Hound is a highly active breed so exercise is necessary for its health, happiness and mental stimulation. Daily exercise is important, and most Ibizans will accept as much as they are given. While lead work is also important, it is essential that some of the daily exercise program gives the hound an

TWO'S COMPANY

One surefire method of increasing your adult dog's exercise plan is to adopt a second dog. If your dog is well socialized, he should take to his new canine pal in no time and soon the two will be giving each other lots of activity and exercise as they play, romp and explore together. Most owners agree that two dogs are hardly much more work than one. If you cannot afford a second dog, get together with a friend or neighbor who has a well-trained dog. Your dog will definitely enjoy the company of a new four-legged playmate.

must be completely dog-proof, and perimeters must be checked regularly to be sure an Ibizan is not working on a new exit route, possibly by means of digging. Don't forget that Ibizans are part jack rabbit, and they will attempt to bounce their way over an average-size fence.

GROOMING YOUR IBIZAN

Ibizan Hounds need little grooming and are generally clean dogs, virtually free from doggy odors. Bathing is needed occasionally, and when selecting a shampoo, take into consideration that some Ibizans have a reaction to insecticides. If ever a product used on the coat causes skin irritation, stop using it immediately and change to one that is milder.

Although the smooth-coated Ibizan may not need as much primping, regular once-overs will keep him looking shiny and healthy.

completely safe. After exercise they should be allowed to settle down quietly for a rest, and remember that following exercise, at least one full hour should always be allowed before feeding, as a precaution against bloat.

Puppies should have only limited exercise during the crucial period of bone growth, so young dogs should be exercised with care.

Because Ibizan Hounds are escapologists, it goes without saying that the yard and run areas

A wire-haired Ibizan should be given a thorough brushing at least once a week to keep his coat looking sharp.

Even when showing an Ibizan Hound, little grooming is required. A light brush, rubber mitt or sisal mitt will remove dead hair. It can also be useful to give the hound a wipe over with a damp cloth, but never leave a dog damp in cold weather or in a draft.

An Ibizan with a wire-haired coat takes a little more work, but this is still minimal compared to many breeds. A thorough weekly brushing is important and dead hairs can be plucked out by hand. However, please take care not to remove too much coat, as this is not a breed that is meant to look like a member of the terrier family.

BATHING

In general, dogs need to be bathed only a few times a year, possibly

more often if your dog gets into something messy. Show dogs are usually bathed before every show, which could be as frequent as weekly, although this depends on the owner. Bathing too frequently can have negative effects on the skin and coat, removing natural oils and causing dryness.

If you give your dog his first bath when he is young, he will become accustomed to the process. Wrestling a dog into the tub or chasing a freshly shampooed dog who has escaped from the bath will be no fun. Most dogs don't naturally enjoy their baths, but you at least want yours to cooperate with you.

Before bathing the dog, have

the items you'll need close at hand. First, decide where you will bathe the dog. You should have a tub or basin with a non-slip surface. Small dogs can even be bathed in a sink. In warm weather, some like to use a portable pool in the yard, although you'll want to make sure your dog doesn't head for the nearest dirt pile following his bath. You will also need a hose or shower spray to wet the coat thoroughly, a shampoo formulated for dogs, absorbent towels and perhaps a blow dryer. Human shampoos are too harsh for dogs' coats and will dry them out.

Before wetting the dog, give him a brush-through to remove any dead hair, dirt and mats. Make sure he is at ease in the tub and have the water at a comfortable temperature. Begin bathing by wetting the coat all the way down to the skin. Massage in the shampoo, keeping it away from his face and eyes. Rinse him thoroughly, again avoiding the eyes and ears, as you don't want

to get water into the ear canals. A thorough rinsing is important, as shampoo residue is drying and itchy to the dog. After rinsing, wrap him in a towel to absorb the initial moisture. You can finish drying with either a towel or a blow dryer on low heat, held at a safe distance from the dog. You should keep the dog indoors and away from drafts until he is completely dry.

Your local pet-supply shop should have all the grooming tools necessary to properly care for your Ibizan Hound and keep him looking in top condition.

NAIL CLIPPING

Having their nails trimmed is not on many dogs' lists of favorite things to do. With this in mind, you will need to accustom your puppy to the procedure at a young age so that he will sit still (well, as still as he can) for his pedicures. Long nails can cause the dog's feet to spread, which is not good for him; likewise, long nails can hurt if they unintentionally scratch, not good for you!

Some dogs' nails are worn down naturally by regular

SUNBLOCK, PLEASE

Because Ibizan Hounds do not have dark pigment, care should be taken that when they are outdoors in strong sunshine their noses and ears to not get burned. They are also very clean and fastidious in their habits, almost cat-like in their cleanliness.

walking on hard surfaces, so the frequency with which you clip depends on your individual dog. Look at his nails from time to time and clip as needed; a good way to know when it's time for a trim is if you hear your dog clicking as he walks across the floor.

There are several types of nail clippers and even electric nail-grinding tools made for dogs; first we'll discuss using the clipper. To start, have your clipper ready and some doggie treats on hand. You want your pup to view his nail-clipping sessions in a positive light, and what better way to convince him than with food? You may want to enlist the help of an assistant to comfort the pup and offer treats as you concentrate on the clipping itself. The guillo-

A pedicure may not be your Ibizan Hound's idea of a good time, but if introduced to the nail clipper as a puppy he will tolerate the procedure.

THE MONTHLY GRIND

If your dog doesn't like the feeling of nail clippers or if you're not comfortable using them, you may wish to try an electric nail grinder. This tool has a small sandpaper disc on the end that rotates to grind the nails down. Some feel that using a grinder reduces the risk of cutting into the quick; this can be true if the tool is used properly. Usually you will be able to tell where the quick is before you get to it. A benefit of the grinder is that it creates a smooth finish on the nails so that there are no ragged edges.

Because the tool makes noise, your dog should be introduced to it before the actual grinding takes place. Turn it on and let your dog hear the noise; turn it off and let him inspect it with you holding it. Use the grinder gently, holding it firmly and progressing a little at a time until you reach the proper length. Look at the nail as you grind so that you do not go too short. Stop at any indication that you are nearing the quick. It will take a few sessions for both you and the puppy to get used to the grinder. If you own a wire-haired Ibizan, make sure that you don't let his hair get tangled in the grinder!

tine-type clipper is thought of by many as the easiest type to use; the nail tip is inserted into the opening, and blades on the top and bottom snip it off in one clip.

Start by grasping the pup's paw; a little pressure on the foot pad causes the nail to extend, making it easier to clip. Clip off a little at a time. If you can see the "quick," which is a blood vessel that runs through each nail, you will know how much to trim, as you do not want to cut into the quick. On that note, if yo u do cut the quick, which will cause bleeding, you can stem the flow of blood with a styptic pencil or other clotting agent. If you mistakenly nip the quick, do not panic or fuss, as this will cause the pup to be afraid. Simply reassure the pup, stop the bleeding and move on to the next nail. Don't be discouraged; you will become a professional canine pedicurist with practice.

You may or may not be able to see the quick, so it's best to just clip off a small bit at a time. If you see a dark dot in the center of the nail, this is the quick and your cue to stop clipping. Tell the puppy he's a "good boy" and offer a piece of treat with each nail. You can also use nail-clipping time to examine the footpads, making sure that they are not dry and cracked and that nothing has become embedded in them.

The nail grinder, the other choice, is many owners' first choice. Accustoming the puppy to the sound of the grinder and sensation of the buzz presents fewer challenges than the clipper, and there's no chance of cutting through the quick. Use the grinder on a low setting and always talk soothingly to your dog. He won't mind his salon visit, and he'll have nicely polished nails as well.

A nail file can also be used to give a good finish to the nails. However, it is important to introduce an Ibizan to routine nail care from an early age, for some can be very awkward about this.

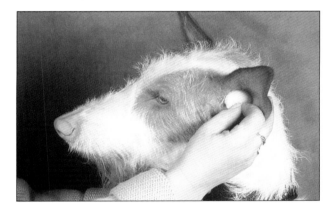

EAR CLEANING
While keeping your dog's ears clean unfortunately will not cause him to "hear" your commands any better, it will protect him from ear infection and ear-mite infestation. In addition, a dog's ears are vulnerable to waxy build-up and to collecting foreign matter from the outdoors. Look in your dog's ears regularly to ensure that they look pink, clean and otherwise healthy. Even if they look fine, an odor in the ears signals a problem and means it's time to call the vet.

To keep your dog's ears clean, wipe them gently with a cotton ball or pad.

A dog's ears should be cleaned regularly; once a week is suggested, and you can do this along with your regular brushing. Using a cotton ball or pad, and never probing into the ear canal, wipe the ear gently. You can use an ear-cleansing liquid or powder available from your vet or pet-supply store; alternatively, you might prefer to use homemade solutions with ingredients like one part white vinegar or one part hydrogen peroxide. Ask your vet about home remedies before you attempt to concoct something on your own!

Keep your dog's ears free of excess hair by plucking it as needed. If done gently, this will be painless for the dog. Look for wax, brown droppings (a sign of

Wiping around the eyes with cotton and a specially made cleansing solution will remove tear stains from your Ibizan's face.

ear mites), redness or any other abnormalities. At the first sign of a problem, contact your vet so that he can prescribe an appropriate medication.

EYE CARE

During grooming sessions, pay extra attention to the condition of your dog's eyes. If the area around the eyes is soiled or if tear staining has occurred, there are various cleaning agents made especially for this purpose. Look at the dog's eyes to make sure no debris has entered; dogs with large eyes and those who spend time outdoors are especially prone to this.

The signs of an eye infection are obvious: mucus, redness, puffiness, scabs or other signs of irritation. If your dog's eyes become infected, the vet will likely prescribe an antibiotic ointment for treatment. If you notice signs of more serious problems, such as opacities in the eye, which usually indicate cataracts, consult the vet at once. Taking time to pay attention to your dog's eyes will alert you in the early stages of any problem so that you can get your dog treatment as soon as possible. You could save your dog's sight!

A CLEAN SMILE

Another essential part of grooming is brushing your dog's teeth and checking his overall oral condition. Studies show that around 80% of dogs experience dental problems by two years of age, and the percentage is higher in older dogs. Therefore it is highly likely that your dog will

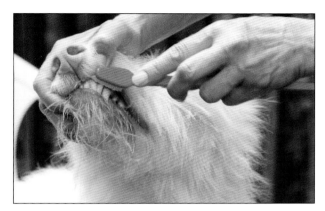

Brushing your Ibizan Hound's teeth regularly at home is important. Accustom your dog to toothbrushing as a puppy, using products designed for dogs.

PRESERVING THOSE PEARLY WHITES

What do you treasure more than the smile of your beloved canine pal? Brushing your dog's teeth is just as important as brushing your own. Neglecting your dog's teeth can lead to tooth loss, periodontal disease and inflamed gums, not to mention bad breath. Can you find the time to brush your dog's teeth every day? If not, you should do so once a week at the very least, though every day is truly the ideal. Your vet should give your dog a thorough dental examination during his annual check-ups.

Pet shops sell terrific tooth-care devices, including specially designed toothbrushes, yummy toothpastes and finger-model brushes. You can use a human toothbrush with soft bristles, but never use human toothpastes, which can damage the dog's enamel. Baking soda is an alternative to doggie toothpastes, but your dog will be more receptive to canine toothpastes with the flavor of liver or hamburger. Make tooth care fun for your dog. Let him think that you're "horsing around" with his mouth. When brushing the dog's teeth, begin with the largest teeth (the canines) and proceed back toward the molars.

have trouble with his teeth and gums unless you are proactive with home dental care.

The most common dental problem in dogs is plaque build-up. If not treated, this causes gum disease, infection and resultant tooth loss. Bacteria from these infections spread throughout the body, affecting the vital organs. Do you need much more convincing to start brushing your dog's teeth? If so, take a good whiff of your dog's breath, and read on.

Fortunately, home dental care is rather easy and convenient for pet owners. Specially formulated canine toothpaste is easy to find. You should use one of these toothpastes, not a product for humans. Some doggie pastes are even available in flavors appealing to dogs. If your dog likes the flavor, he will tolerate the process better, making things much easier for you! Doggie toothbrushes come in different sizes and are

Do not use human toothpaste on your Ibizan! Doggie toothpastes come in a variety of flavors that your hound will love.

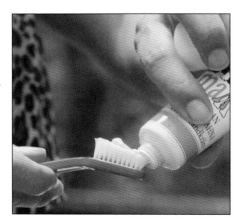

designed to fit the contour of a canine mouth. Rubber fingertip brushes fit right on one of your fingers and have rubber nodes to clean the teeth and massage the gums. This may be easier to handle, as it is akin to rubbing your dog's teeth with your finger.

As with other grooming tasks, accustom your Ibizan Hound pup to his dental care early on. Start gently, for a few minutes at a time, so that he gets used to the feel of the brush and to your handling his mouth. Offer praise and petting so that he looks at tooth-care time as a time when he gets extra love and attention. The routine should become second nature; he may not like it, but he should at least tolerate it.

Aside from brushing, offer dental toys to your dog and feed crunchy biscuits, which help to minimize plaque. Rope toys have the added benefit of acting like floss as the dog chews. At your

adult dog's yearly check-ups, the vet will likely perform a thorough tooth scraping as well as a complete check for any problems. Proper care of your dog's teeth will ensure that you will enjoy

PUPPY LE PEW

On that ill-fated day when your puppy insults the neighborhood skunk by calling him a weasel, you will likely have the unhappy chore of "de-skunking" your dog. Skunks are not afraid of puppies (or even full-sized dogs) and will take on an approaching "predator." The skunk's spray is a nasty compound called thiols, a thick, oily liquid that can also be found in decaying flesh or feces. After the skunk hisses, growls and does his "don't-mess-with-me" dance, he sprays the unsuspecting canine.

The age-old remedy was to bathe a "skunked" dog in tomato juice, but thanks to chemist Paul Krebaum, you can put away your can opener. Krebaum provides us with this easy and effective recipe to deodorize your stinky puppy: 1 quart 3% hydrogen peroxide; 1/4 cup baking soda; and 1 teaspoon liquid dish detergent. Work the soapy formula into the dog's coat and keep it out of the dog's eyes. Rinse the dog thoroughly after the bath. Do not make this formula and attempt to bottle it—it will explode! Incidentally, the skunk is in fact in the weasel family, but there's no sense arguing with the nasty-tempered mouse-eating fellow.

your dog's smile for many years to come. The next time your dog goes to give you a hello kiss, you'll be glad you spent the time caring for his teeth.

The Other End

Dogs sometime have troubles with their anal glands, which are sacs located beside the anal vent. These should empty when a dog has normal bowel movements; if they don't, they can become full or impacted, causing discomfort. Owners often are alarmed to see their dogs scooting across the floor, dragging their behinds behind, this is just a dog's attempt to empty the glands himself.

Some brave owners attempt to evacuate their dogs' anal glands themselves during grooming, but no one will tell you that this is a pleasant task. Thus, many owners prefer to make the trip to the vet to have the vet take care of the problem; owners whose dogs visit a groomer can have this done by the groomer if he offers this as part of his services. Regardless, don't neglect the dog's other end in your home-care routine. Look for scooting, licking or other signs of discomfort "back there" to ascertain whether the anal glands need to be emptied.

IDENTIFICATION FOR YOUR IBIZAN HOUND

You love your Ibizan Hound and want to keep him safe. Of course you take every precaution to prevent his escaping from the yard or becoming lost or stolen.

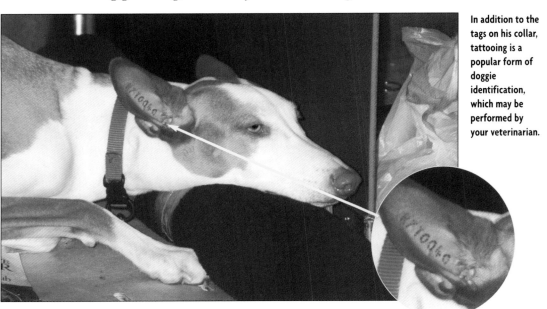

In addition to the tags on his collar, tattooing is a popular form of doggie identification, which may be performed by your veterinarian.

PET OR STRAY?
Besides the obvious benefit of providing your contact information to whoever finds your lost dog, an ID tag makes your dog more approachable and more likely to be recovered. A strange dog wandering the neighborhood without a collar and tags will look like a stray, while the collar and tags indicate that the dog is someone's pet. Even if the ID tags become detached from the collar, the collar alone will make a person more likely to pick up the dog.

You have a sturdy high fence and you always keep your dog on lead when out and about in public places. If your dog is not properly identified, however, you are overlooking a major aspect of his safety. We hope to never be in a situation where our dog is missing, but we should practice prevention in the unfortunate case that this happens; identification greatly increases the chances of your dog's being returned to you.

There are several ways to identify your dog. First, the traditional dog tag should be a staple in your dog's wardrobe, attached to his everyday collar. Tags can be made of sturdy plastic and various metals and should include your contact information so that a person who finds the dog can get in touch with you right away to arrange his return. Many people today enjoy the wide range of decorative tags available, so have fun and create a tag to match your dog's personality. Of course, it is important that the tag stays on the collar, so have a secure "O" ring attachment; you also can explore the type of tag that slides right onto the collar.

In addition to the ID tag, which every dog should wear even if identified by another method, two other forms of identification have become popular: microchipping and tattooing. In microchipping, a tiny scannable chip is painlessly inserted under the dog's skin. The number is registered to you so that, if your lost dog turns up at a clinic or shelter, the chip can be scanned to retrieve your contact information.

The advantage of the microchip is that it is a permanent form of ID, but there are some factors to consider. Several different companies make microchips, and not all are compatible with the others' scanning devices. It's best to find a company with a universal microchip that can be read by scanners made by other companies as well. It won't do any good to have the dog chipped if the information cannot be retrieved. Also, not every humane society, shelter and clinic is equipped with a scanner, although more and more facilities are equipping themselves. In fact, many shelters microchip dogs that they adopt out to new homes.

Because the microchip is not visible to the eye, the dog must wear a tag that states that he is microchipped so that whoever picks him up will know to have him scanned. He of course also should have a tag with your contact information in case his chip cannot be read. Humane societies and veterinary clinics offer this service, which is usually very affordable.

Though less popular than microchipping, tattooing is another permanent method of ID for dogs. Most vets perform this service, and there are also clinics that perform dog tattooing. This is also an affordable procedure and one that will not cause much discomfort for the dog. It is best to put the tattoo in a visible area,

such as the ear, to deter theft. It is sad to say that there are cases of dogs' being stolen and sold to research laboratories, but such laboratories will not accept tattooed dogs.

To ensure that the tattoo is effective in aiding your dog's return to you, the tattoo number must be registered with a national organization. That way, when someone finds a tattooed dog a phone call to the registry will quickly match the dog with his owner.

BOARDING

Today there are many options for dog owners who need someone to care for their dogs in certain circumstances. While many think of boarding their dogs as something to do when away on

If possible, check if your breeder will board your Ibizan. This way you can trust that your hound is in good hands, and he can meet some family members.

Make some visits to kennels in your area to meet the staff, see the premises and learn about their services, so you know which facility you will use before you even need it.

vacation, many others use the services of doggie "daycare" facilities, dropping their dogs off to spend the day while they are at work. Many of these facilities offer both long-term and daily care. Many go beyond just boarding and cater to all sorts of needs, with on-site grooming,

DOGGONE!

Wendy Ballard is the editor and publisher of the *DogGone*™ newsletter, which comes out bi-monthly and features fun articles by dog owners who love to travel with their dogs. The newsletter includes information about fun places to go with your dogs, including popular vacation spots, dog-friendly hotels, parks, campgrounds, resorts, etc., as well as interesting activities to do with your dog, such as flyball, agility and much more. You can subscribe to the publication by contacting the publisher at PO Box 651155, Vero Beach, FL 32965-1155.

veterinary care, training classes and even "web-cams" where owners can log onto the Internet and check out what their dogs are up to. Most dogs enjoy the activity and time spent with other dogs.

Before you need to use such a service, check out the ones in your area. Make visits to see the facilities, meet the staff, discuss fees and available services and see whether this is a place where you think your dog will be happy. It is best to do your research in advance so that you're not stuck at the last minute, forced into making a rushed decision without knowing whether the kennel that you've chosen meets your standards. You also can check with your vet's office to see whether they offer boarding for their clients or can recommend a good kennel in the area.

The kennel will need to see proof of your dog's health records and vaccinations so as not to spread illness from dog to dog. Your dog also will need proper identification. Owners usually experience some separation anxiety the first time they have to leave their dog in someone else's care, so it's reassuring to know that the kennel you choose is run by experienced, caring, true dog people.

IBIZAN HOUND

Few dogs in the world are as tuned into their senses as the Ibizan Hound. This remarkable hound uses his senses of sight, sound and scent to their full capacities, at least as far as you can imagine. Pet owners must realize that they are living with a dog who was bred to chase everything and anything he can see, hear and smell. Often when you think he's twittering with excitement over imaginary quarry, a rabbit will hop in the distance and your hound will break the speed limit to get to it.

Keeping this in mind, training the Ibizan Hound requires an owner who is sensitive to his dog's abilities. Ibizans should never be over-handled; in fact, they resent heavy handling and prefer to work things out on their own. Ibizans in training classes often look distracted, unhappy and difficult. They resist traditional methods, despise repetition and should never be yanked about on a leash.

Their historical usage of hunting small animals without direction from a hunter has made this breed independent. The Ibizan is a solo act, preferring to make decisions on his own, similar to the great flock guard breeds who worked without the assistance or direction of a shepherd.

As far as training is concerned, Ibizans aren't terribly interested, though they are keen to play games. Given the breed's intense prey drive, playing usually means chasing. He'll happily chase his owner, the neighbor's cat or another dog. His favorite game involves out-running his playmates, as he's rarely lost a race. He'll run for the

A well-trained Ibizan Hound will be a joy to take with you wherever you go and will be happy to be engaged in some fun activities.

joy of running, and once he's going over 5 miles per hour, his miraculous ears shut off. Here is a bouncing, pouncing, fun-loving hound who lives to entertain his family and friends.

Fortunately Ibizan Hounds are chow hounds and can be readily motivated with food treats. Soft, moist, smelly treats work best. Often bribery can overcome a dog's desire to wander away from his owner, though you should never trust an Ibizan Hound off leash unless you are in a completely, safely fenced area. A potential disaster awaits for the Ibizan Hound in hurried pursuit for the hare across the freeway! Keep the dog on leash, no matter how well trained you think he is. You can use the dog's prey drive to your advantage in training, but you can never erase it from the animal.

Gaining your Ibizan's respect and trust comes from gentle handling and intense socialization. A dog that trusts you becomes a more confident and less reluctant student. When the Ibizan is getting the upper hand and your frustration level is rising, skip training for the day and play a game that the dog loves. Discipline must be doled out orally and never physically. Correct the dog firmly but never strike the dog; you will never regain the trust of an Ibizan you abuse. Ibizans are sensitive and hate to be ignored. When your dog is disinclined to work with you,

Training a dog with show potential begins in puppyhood. Along with the basic commands, the pup will need to learn to stand and stay for examination by the judge.

give him the "cold shoulder" for 15 minutes. Your displeasure will register, and he'll be more willing to cooperate for the next lesson.

BASIC TRAINING PRINCIPLES: PUPPY VS. ADULT

There's a big difference between training an adult dog and training a young puppy. With a young puppy, everything is new. At eight to ten weeks of age, he will be experiencing many things, and he has nothing with which to compare these experiences. Up to this point, he has been with his dam and littermates, not one-on-one with people except in his interactions with his breeder and visitors to the litter.

When you first bring the puppy home, he is eager to please you. This means that he accepts doing things your way. During the next couple of months, he will absorb the basis of everything he needs to know for the rest of his life. This early age is even referred to as the "sponge" stage. After that, for the next 18 months, it's up to you to reinforce good manners by building on the foundation that you've established. Once your puppy is reliable in basic commands and behavior and has reached the appropriate age, you may gradually introduce him to some of the interesting sports, games and activities available to pet owners and their dogs.

THE RIGHT START

The best advice for a potential dog owner is to start with the very best puppy that money can buy. Don't shop around for a bargain in the newspaper. You're buying a companion, not a used car or a second-hand appliance. The purchase price of the dog represents a very significant part of the investment, but this is indeed a very small sum compared to the expenses of maintaining the dog in good health. If you purchase a well-bred healthy and sound puppy, you will be starting right. An unhealthy puppy can cost you thousands of dollars in unnecessary veterinary expenses and, possibly, a fortune in heartbreak as well.

Raising your puppy is a family affair. Each member of the family must know what rules to set forth for the puppy and how to use the same one-word commands to mean exactly the same thing every time. Even if yours is a large family, one person will soon be considered by the pup to be the leader, the alpha person in his pack, the "boss" who must be obeyed. Often that highly regarded person turns out to be the one who feeds the puppy. Food ranks very high on the puppy's list of important things. That's why your puppy is rewarded with small treats along with verbal praise when he responds to you correctly. As the puppy learns to do what you want him to do, the food rewards are gradually eliminated and only the praise remains. If you were to keep up with the food treats, you could have two problems on your hands—an obese dog and a beggar.

Your Ibizan Hound will look to you as his "pack leader," and it is your responsibility to provide proper guidance.

PHOTOGRAPHY BY CAROL BEUCHAT.

Training begins the minute your Ibizan Hound puppy steps through the doorway of your home, so don't make the mistake of putting the puppy on the floor and telling him by your actions to "Go for it! Run wild!" Even if this is your first puppy, you must act as if you know what you're doing: be the boss. An uncertain pup may be terrified to move, while a bold one will be ready to take you at your word and start plotting to destroy the house! Before you collected your puppy, you decided where his own special place would be, and that's where to put him when you first arrive home. Give him a house tour after he has investigated his area and had a nap and a bathroom "pit stop."

It's worth mentioning here that, if you've adopted an adult dog that is completely trained to your liking, lucky you! You're off the hook! However, if that dog spent his life up to this point in a kennel, or even in a good home but without any real training, be prepared to tackle the job ahead. A dog three years of age or older with no previous training cannot be blamed for not knowing what he was never taught. While the dog is trying to understand and learn your rules, at the same time he has to unlearn many of his previously self-taught habits and general view of the world.

Working with a professional trainer will speed up your progress with an adopted adult dog. You'll need patience, too. Some new rules may be close to impossible for the dog to accept. After all, he's been successful so far by doing everything his way! (Patience again.) He may agree with your instruction for a few days and then slip back into his old ways, so you must be just as consistent and understanding in your teaching as you would be with a puppy. (More patience needed yet again!) Your dog has to learn to pay attention to your voice, your family, the daily routine, new smells, new sounds and, in some cases, even a new climate.

One of the most important things to find out about a newly adopted adult dog is his reaction to children (yours and others), strangers and your friends, and how he acts upon meeting other dogs. If he was not socialized with dogs as a puppy, this could be a major problem. This does not mean that he's a "bad" dog, a vicious dog or an aggressive dog; rather, it means that he has no idea how to read another dog's body language. There's no way for him to tell whether the other dog is a friend or foe. Survival instinct takes over, telling him to attack first and ask questions later. This definitely calls for professional help and, even then, may not be a behavior that can be corrected

> **OUR CANINE KIDS**
> "Everything I learned about parenting, I learned from my dog." How often adults recognize that their parenting skills are mere extensions of the education they acquired while caring for their dogs. Many owners refer to their dogs as their "kids" and treat their canine companions like real members of the family. Surveys indicate that a majority of dog owners talk to their dogs regularly, celebrate their dogs' birthdays and purchase Christmas gifts for their dogs. Another survey shows that dog owners take their dogs to the veterinarian more frequently than they visit their own physicians.

100% reliably (or even at all). If you have a puppy, this is why it is so very important to introduce your young puppy properly to other puppies and "dog-friendly" adult dogs.

HOUSE-TRAINING YOUR IBIZAN HOUND

Dogs are tactility-oriented when it comes to house-training. In other words, they respond to the surface on which they are given approval to eliminate. The choice is yours (the dog's version is in parentheses): The lawn (including the neighbors' lawns)? A bare patch of earth under a tree (where people like to sit and relax in the summertime)? Concrete steps or

EXTRA! EXTRA!

The headlines read: "Puppy Piddles Here!" Breeders commonly use newspapers to line their whelping pens, so puppies learn to associate newspapers with relieving themselves. Do not use newspapers to line your pup's crate, as this will signal to your puppy that it is OK to urinate in his crate. If you choose to paper-train your puppy, you will layer newspapers on a section of the floor near the door he uses to go outside. You should encourage the puppy to use the papers to relieve himself, and bring him there whenever you see him getting ready to go. Little by little, you will reduce the size of the newspaper-covered area so that the puppy will learn to relieve himself "on the other side of the door."

patio (all sidewalks, garages and basement floors)? The curbside (watch out for cars)? A small area of crushed stone in a corner of the yard (mine!)? The latter is the best choice if you can manage it, because it will remain strictly for the dog's use and is easy to keep clean.

You can start out with paper-training indoors and switch over to an outdoor surface as the puppy matures and gains control over his need to eliminate. For the naysayers, don't worry—this won't mean that the dog will soil on every piece of newspaper lying around the house. You are training him to go outside, remember? Starting out by paper-training often is the only choice for a city dog.

WHEN YOUR PUPPY'S "GOT TO GO"
Your puppy's need to relieve himself is seemingly non-stop, but signs of improvement will be seen each week. From 8 to 10 weeks old, the puppy will have to be taken outside every time he wakes up, about 10-15 minutes after every meal and after every period of play—all day long, from first thing in the morning until his bedtime! That's a total of ten or more trips per day to teach the puppy where it's okay to relieve himself. With that schedule in mind, you can see that house-training a young puppy is not a part-time job. It requires someone to be home all day.

If that seems overwhelming or impossible, do a little planning. For example, plan to pick up your puppy at the start of a vacation period. If you can't get home in the middle of the day, plan to hire a dog-sitter or ask a neighbor to come over to take the pup outside, feed him his lunch and then take him out again about ten or so minutes after he's eaten. Also make arrangements with that or another person to be your "emergency" contact if you have to stay late on the job. Remind yourself—repeatedly—that this hectic schedule improves as the puppy gets older.

HOME WITHIN A HOME

Your Ibizan Hound puppy needs to be confined to one secure, puppy-proof area when no one is able to watch his every move. Generally, the kitchen is the place of choice because the floor is washable. Likewise, it's a busy family area that will accustom the pup to a variety of noises, everything from pots and pans to the telephone, blender and dishwasher. He will also be enchanted by the smell of your cooking (and will never be critical when you burn something). An exercise pen (also called an "ex-pen," a puppy version of a playpen) within the room of choice is an excellent means of confinement for a young pup. He can see out and has a certain

When potty-training your Ibizan, accompany him to his outdoor "spot" while he is on leash.

amount of space in which to run about, but he is safe from dangerous things like electrical cords, heating units, trash baskets or open kitchen-supply cabinets. Place the pen where the puppy will not get a blast of heat or air conditioning.

In the pen, you can put a few toys, his bed (which can be his crate if the dimensions of pen and crate are compatible) and a few layers of newspaper in one small corner, just in case. A water bowl can be hung at a convenient height on the side of the ex-pen so it won't become a splashing pool for an innovative puppy. His food dish can go on the floor, next to but not under the water bowl.

Crates are something that pet owners are at last getting used to for their dogs. Wild or domestic canines have always preferred to sleep in den-like safe spots, and that is exactly what the crate provides. How often have you seen adult dogs that choose to sleep under a table or chair even

DAILY SCHEDULE

How many relief trips does your puppy need per day? A puppy up to the age of 14 weeks will need to go outside about 8 to 12 times per day! You will have to take the pup out any time he starts sniffing around the floor or turning in small circles, as well as after naps, meals, games and lessons or whenever he's released from his crate. Once the puppy is 14 to 22 weeks of age, he will require only 6 to 8 relief trips. At the ages of 22 to 32 weeks, the puppy will require about 5 to 7 trips. Adult dogs typically require 4 relief trips per day, in the morning, afternoon, evening and late at night.

times. At night, after he's been outside, he should sleep in his crate. The crate may be kept in his designated area at night or, if you want to be sure to hear those wake-up yips in the morning, put the crate in a corner of your bedroom. However, don't make any response whatsoever to whining or crying. If he's completely ignored, he'll settle down and get to sleep.

Good bedding for a young puppy is an old folded bath towel or an old blanket, something that is easily washable and disposable if necessary ("accidents" will happen!). Never put newspaper in the puppy's crate. Also those old ideas about adding a clock to replace his mother's heartbeat or a hot-water bottle to replace her warmth, are just that—old ideas. The clock could drive the puppy nuts, and the hot-water bottle could end up as a very soggy waterbed! An extremely good breeder would have introduced your puppy to the crate by letting two pups sleep together for a couple of nights, followed by several nights alone. How thankful you will be if you found that breeder!

Safe toys in the pup's crate or area will keep him occupied, but monitor their condition closely. Discard any toys that show signs of being chewed to bits. Squeaky parts, bits of stuffing or plastic or any other small pieces can cause

though they have full run of the house? It's the den connection.

In your "happy" voice, use the word "Crate" every time you put the pup into his den. If he's new to a crate, toss in a small biscuit for him to chase the first few intestinal blockage or possibly choking if swallowed.

PROGRESSING WITH POTTY-TRAINING
After you've taken your puppy out and he has relieved himself in the area you've selected, he can have some free time with the family as long as there is someone responsible for watching him. That doesn't mean just someone in the same room who is watching TV or busy on the computer, but one person who is doing nothing other than keeping an eye on the pup, playing with him on the floor and helping him understand his position in the pack.

This first taste of freedom will let you begin to set the house rules. If you don't want the dog on the furniture, now is the time to prevent his first attempts to jump up onto the couch. The word to use in this case is "Off," not "Down." "Down" is the word you will use to teach the down position, which is something entirely different.

Most corrections at this stage come in the form of simply distracting the puppy. Instead of telling him "No" for "Don't chew the carpet," distract the chomping puppy with a toy and he'll forget about the carpet.

As you are playing with the pup, do not forget to watch him closely and pay attention to his body language. Whenever you see him begin to circle or sniff, take

the puppy outside to relieve himself. If you are paper-training, put him back into his confined area on the newspapers. In either case, praise him as he eliminates while he actually is in the act of relieving himself. Three seconds after he has finished is too late! You'll be praising him for running toward you, picking up a toy or whatever he may be doing at that moment, and that's not what you want to be praising him for. Timing is a vital tool in all dog training. Use it!

Remove soiled newspapers immediately and replace them with clean ones. You may want to take a small piece of soiled paper and place it in the middle of the new clean papers, as the scent will attract him to that spot when it's time to go again. That scent attraction is why it's so important to clean up any messes made in

While an exercise pen is suitable for Ibizans as puppies, it will not confine an adult Ibizan, who can easily leap to freedom.

An Ibizan should only be allowed off leash to go to the bathroom in a yard with a fence that will be able to contain this escapologist.

him to his spot. Now comes the hard part—hard for you, that is. Just stand there until he urinates and defecates. Move him a few feet in one direction or another if he's just sitting there looking at you, but remember that this is neither playtime nor time for a walk. This is strictly a business trip! Then, as he circles and squats (remember your timing!), give him a quiet "Good dog" as praise. If you start to jump for joy, ecstatic over his performance, he'll do one of two things: either he will stop mid-stream, as it were, or he'll do it again for you—in the house—and expect you to be just as delighted!

Give him five minutes or so and, if he doesn't go in that time, take him back indoors to his confined area and try again in another ten minutes, or immediately if you see him sniffing and circling. By careful observation, you'll soon work out a successful schedule.

Accidents, by the way, are just that—accidents. Clean them up quickly and thoroughly, without comment, after the puppy has

the house by using a product specially made to eliminate the odor of dog urine and droppings. Regular household cleansers won't do the trick. Pet shops sell the best pet deodorizers. Invest in the largest container you can find.

Scent attraction eventually will lead your pup to his chosen spot outdoors; this is the basis of outdoor training. When you take your puppy outside to relieve himself, use a one-word command such as "Outside" or "Go-potty" (that's one word to the puppy!) as you attach his leash. Then lead

CREATURES OF HABIT
Canine behaviorists and trainers aptly describe dogs as "creatures of habit," meaning that dogs respond to structure in their daily lives and welcome a routine. Do not interpret this to mean that dogs enjoy endless repetition in their training sessions. Dogs get bored just as humans do. Keep training sessions interesting and exciting. Vary the commands and the locations in which you practice. Give short breaks for play in between lessons. A bored student will never be the best performer in the class.

been taken outside to finish his business and then put back into his area or crate. If you witness an accident in progress, say "No!" in a stern voice and get the pup outdoors immediately. No punishment is needed. You and your puppy are just learning each other's language, and sometimes it's easy to miss a puppy's message. Chalk it up to experience and watch more closely from now on.

KEEPING THE PACK ORDERLY

Discipline is a form of training that brings order to life. For example, military discipline is what allows the soldiers in an army to work as one. Discipline is a form of teaching and, in dogs, is the basis of how the successful pack operates. Each member knows his place in the pack and all respect the leader, or alpha dog. It is essential for your puppy that you establish this type of relationship, with you as the alpha, or leader. It is a form of social coexistence that all canines recognize and accept. Discipline, therefore, is never to be confused with punishment. When you teach your puppy how you want him to behave, and he behaves properly and you praise him for it, you are disciplining him with a form of positive reinforcement.

For a dog, rewards come in the form of praise, a smile, a cheerful tone of voice, a few

POTTY COMMAND

Most dogs love to please their masters; there are no bounds to what dogs will do to make their owners happy. The potty command is a good example of this theory. If toileting on command makes the master happy, then more power to him. Puppies will obligingly piddle if it really makes their keepers smile. Some owners can be creative about which word they will use to command their dogs to relieve themselves. Some popular choices are "Potty," "Tinkle," "Piddle," "Let's go," "Hurry up" and "Toilet." Give the command every time your puppy goes into position and the puppy will begin to associate his business with the command.

friendly pats or a rub of the ears. Rewards are also small food treats. Obviously, that does not mean bits of regular dog food. Instead, treats are very small bits of special things like cheese or pieces of soft dog treats. The idea is to reward the dog with something very small that he can taste and swallow, providing instant positive reinforcement. If he has to take time to chew the treat, by the time he is finished he will have forgotten what he did to earn it.

Your puppy should never be physically punished. The displeasure shown on your face and in your voice is sufficient to signal to the pup that he has done something wrong. He wants to please everyone higher up on the social ladder, especially his leader, so a scowl and harsh voice will take care of the error.

Before training begins, your Ibizan will need to be properly accustomed to his leash and collar.

Growling out the word "Shame!" when the pup is caught in the act of doing something wrong is better than the repetitive "No." Some dogs hear "No" so often that they begin to think it's their name! By the way, do not use the dog's name when you're correcting him. His name is reserved to get his attention for something pleasant about to take place.

There are punishments that have nothing to do with you. For example, your dog may think that chasing cats is one reason for his existence. You can try to stop it as much as you like but without success, because it's such fun for the dog. But one good hissing, spitting swipe of a cat's claws across the dog's nose will put an end to the game forever. Intervene only when your dog's eyeball is seriously at risk. Cat scratches can cause permanent damage to an innocent but annoying puppy.

PUPPY KINDERGARTEN

COLLAR AND LEASH
Before you begin your Ibizan Hound puppy's education, he must be used to his collar and leash. Choose a collar for your puppy that is secure, but not heavy or bulky. He won't enjoy training if he's uncomfortable. A flat buckle collar is fine for

The reward of training your Ibizan Hound is an intelligent, alert, personable and multi-talented canine companion.

LEASH TRAINING

House-training and leash training go hand in hand, literally. When taking your puppy outside to do his business, lead him there on his leash. Unless an emergency potty run is called for, do not whisk the puppy up into your arms and take him outside. If you have a fenced yard, you have the advantage of letting the puppy loose to go out, but it's better to put the dog on the leash and take him to his designated place in the yard until he is reliably house-trained. Taking the puppy for a walk is the best way to house-train a dog. The dog will associate the walk with his time to relieve himself, and the exercise of walking stimulates the dog's bowels and bladder. Dogs that are not trained to relieve themselves on a walk may hold it until they get back home, which of course defeats half the purpose of the walk.

A lightweight 6-foot woven cotton or nylon training leash is preferred by most trainers because it is easy to fold up in your hand and comfortable to hold because there is a certain amount of give to it. There are lessons where the dog will start off 6 feet away from you at the end of the leash. The leash used to take the puppy outside to relieve himself is shorter because you don't want him to roam away from his area. The shorter leash will also be the one to use when you walk the puppy.

If you've been wise enough to enroll in a puppy kindergarten training class, suggestions will be made as to the best collar and leash for your young puppy. I say "wise" because your puppy will be in a class with puppies in his age range (up to five months old) of all breeds and sizes. It's the perfect way for him to learn the right way (and the wrong way) to interact with other dogs as well as

everyday wear and for initial puppy training. For older dogs, there are several types of training collars such as the martingale, which is a double loop that tightens slightly around the neck, or the head collar, which is similar to a horse's halter. Do not use a chain choke collar unless you have been specifically shown how to put it on and how to use it. You may not be disposed to use a chain choke collar even if your breeder has told you that it's suitable for your Ibizan Hound.

Even when properly trained, keep your Ibizans on leash when out and about.

their people. You cannot teach your puppy how to interpret another dog's sign language. For a first-time puppy owner, these socialization classes are invaluable. For experienced dog owners, they are a real boon to further training.

ATTENTION

You've been using the dog's name since the minute you collected him from the breeder, so you should be able to get his attention by saying his name—with a big smile and in an excited tone of voice. His response will be the puppy equivalent of "Here I am! What are we going to do?" Your immediate response (if you haven't guessed by now) is "Good

> ## BASIC PRINCIPLES OF DOG TRAINING
> 1. Start training early. A young puppy is ready, willing and able.
> 2. Timing is your all-important tool. Praise at the exact time that the dog responds correctly. Pay close attention.
> 3. Patience is almost as important as timing!
> 4. Repeat! The same word has to mean the same thing every time.
> 5. In the beginning, praise all correct behavior verbally, along with treats and petting.

dog." Rewarding him at the moment he pays attention to you teaches him the proper way to respond when he hears his name.

EXERCISES FOR A BASIC CANINE EDUCATION

THE SIT EXERCISE

There are several ways to teach the puppy to sit. The first one is to catch him whenever he is about to sit and, as his backside nears the floor, say "Sit, good dog!" That's positive reinforcement and, if your timing is sharp, he will learn that what he's doing at that second is connected to your saying "Sit" and that you think he's clever for doing it!

Another method is to start with the puppy on his leash in front of you. Show him a treat in

It may help to teach the sit by first guiding the dog into the correct position a few times. Praise him when he assumes a proper sit with your help, and soon he will get the idea and do it on his own.

the palm of your right hand. Bring your hand up under his nose and, almost in slow motion, move your hand up and back so his nose goes up in the air and his head tilts back as he follows the treat in your hand. At that point, he will have to either sit or fall over, so as his back legs buckle under, say "Sit, good dog," and then give him the treat and lots of praise. You may have to begin with your hand lightly running up his chest, actually lifting his chin up until he sits. Some (usually older) dogs require gentle pressure on their hindquarters with the left hand, in which case the dog should be on your left side. Puppies generally do not appreciate this physical dominance.

After a few times, you should be able to show the dog a treat in the open palm of your hand, raise your hand waist-high as you say "Sit" and have him sit. You will thereby have taught him two things at the same time. Both the verbal command and the motion of the hand are signals for the sit. Your puppy is watching you almost more than he is listening to you, so what you do is just as important as what you say.

Don't save any of these drills only for training sessions. Use them as much as possible at odd times during a normal day. The dog should always sit before being given his food dish. He should sit to let you go through a doorway

READY, SIT, GO!
On your marks, get set: train! Most professional trainers agree that the sit command is the place to start your dog's formal education. Sitting is a natural posture for most dogs, and they respond to the sit exercise willingly and readily. For every lesson, begin with the sit command so that you start out on a successful note; likewise, you should practice the sit command at the end of every lesson as well, because you always want to end on a high note.

first, when the doorbell rings or when you stop to speak to someone on the street.

THE DOWN EXERCISE
Before beginning to teach the down command, you must

your right hand. Place it at the end of the pup's nose and steadily move your hand down and forward along the ground. Hold the leash to prevent a sudden lunge for the food. As the puppy goes into the down position, say "Down" very gently.

The difficulty with this exercise is twofold: it's both the submissive aspect and the fact that most people say the word "Down" as if they were drill

The down position will not be a favorite of your Ibizan Hound, but he will assume the position with some coaxing, and a treat will certainly help.

consider how the dog feels about this exercise. To him, "down" is a submissive position. Being flat on the floor with you standing over him is not his idea of fun. It's up to you to let him know that, while it may not be fun, the reward of your approval is worth his effort.

Start with the puppy on your left side in a sit position. Hold the leash right above his collar in your left hand. Have an extra-special treat, such as a small piece of cooked chicken or hot dog, in

DOWN

"Down" is a harsh-sounding word and a submissive posture in dog body language, thus presenting two obstacles in teaching the down command. When the dog is about to flop down on his own, tell him "Good down." Pups that are not good about being handled learn better by having food lowered in front of them. A dog that trusts you can be gently guided into position. When you give the command "Down," be sure to say it sweetly!

sergeants in charge of recruits! So issue the command sweetly, give him the treat and have the pup maintain the down position for several seconds. If he tries to get up immediately, place your hands on his shoulders and press down gently, giving him a very quiet "Good dog." As you progress with this lesson, increase the "down time" until he will hold it until you say "Okay" (his cue for release). Practice this one in the house at various times throughout the day.

By increasing the length of time during which the dog must maintain the down position, you'll find many uses for it. For example, he can lie at your feet in the vet's office or anywhere that both of you have to wait, when you are on the phone, while the family is eating and so forth. If you progress to training for competitive obedience, he'll already be all set for the exercise called the "long down."

THE STAY EXERCISE

You can teach your Ibizan Hound to stay in the sit, down and stand positions. To teach the sit/stay, have the dog sit on your left side. Hold the leash at waist level in your left hand and let the dog know that you have a treat in your closed right hand. Step forward

Distance between the handler and dog is gradually increased in the stay exercise. It is best to be in a fenced area or to use an extra-long lead, just in case something besides the lesson captures your Ibizan Hound's interest.

Of course your Ibizan will want his treat, but he gets it only if he remains in the stay position until you reach him.

on your right foot as you say "Stay." Immediately turn and stand directly in front of the dog, keeping your right hand up high so he'll keep his eye on the treat hand and maintain the sit position for a count of five. Return to your original position and offer the reward.

Increase the length of the sit/stay each time until the dog can hold it for at least 30 seconds without moving. After about a week of success, move out on your right foot and take two steps before turning to face the dog. Give the "Stay" hand signal (left palm back toward the dog's head) as you leave. He gets the treat

when you return and he holds the sit/stay. Increase the distance that you walk away from him before turning until you reach the length of your training leash. But don't rush it! Go back to the beginning if he moves before he should. No matter what the lesson, never be upset by having to back up for a few days. The repetition and practice are what will make your dog reliable in these commands. It won't do any good to move on to something more difficult if the command is not mastered at the easier levels. Above all, even if you do get frustrated, never let your puppy know! Always keep a positive, upbeat attitude during training, which will transmit to your dog for positive results.

The down/stay is taught in the same way once the dog is completely reliable and steady with the down command. Again, don't rush it. With the dog in the down position on your left side, step out on your right foot as you say "Stay." Return by walking around in back of the dog and into your original position. While you are training, it's okay to murmur something like "Hold on" to encourage him to stay put. When the dog will stay without moving when you are at a distance of 3 or 4 feet, begin to increase the length of time before you return. Be sure he holds the down on your return until you say "Okay." At that point, he gets his treat—just so he'll remember for next time that it's not over until it's over.

THE COME EXERCISE

No command is more important to the safety of your Ibizan Hound than "Come." It is what you should say every single time you see the puppy running toward you: "Iggy, come! Good dog." During playtime, run a few feet away from the puppy and turn and tell him to "Come" as he is already running to you. You can go so far as to teach your puppy two things at once if you squat down and hold out your arms. As the pup gets close to you and you're saying "Good dog," bring your right arm in about waist high. Now he's also learning the hand signal, an excellent device should you be on the phone when you need to get him to come to you! You'll also both be one step ahead when you enter obedience classes.

When the puppy responds to your well-timed "Come," try it with the puppy on the training leash. This time, catch him off guard, while he's sniffing a leaf or watching a bird: "Iggy, come!" You may have to pause for a split second after his name to be sure you have his attention. If the puppy shows any sign of confusion, give the leash a mild jerk and take a couple of steps backward. Do not repeat the command. In this case, you should say "Good come" as he reaches you.

That's the number-one rule of training. Each command word is given just once. Anything more is nagging. You'll also notice that all commands are one word only. Even when they are actually two words, you say them as one.

COME AND GET IT!

The come command is your dog's safety signal. Until he is 99% perfect in responding, don't use the come command if you cannot enforce it. Practice on leash with treats or squeakers, or whenever the dog is running to you. Never call him to come to you if he is to be corrected for a misdemeanor. Reward the dog with a treat and happy praise whenever he comes to you.

Mastering the heel command will come in handy if one of your goals is to gait your Ibizan Hound around the show ring.

Never call the dog to come to you—with or without his name—if you are angry or intend to correct him for some misbehavior. When correcting the pup, you go to him. Your dog must always connect "Come" with something pleasant and with your approval; then you can rely on his response.

FROM HEEL TO ETERNITY
To begin, step away from the dog, who is in the sit position, on your left foot. That tells the dog you aren't going anywhere. Turn and stand directly in front of him so he won't be tempted to follow. Two seconds is a long, long time to your dog, so increase the time for which he's expected to stay only in short increments. Don't force it. When practicing the heel exercise, your dog will sit at your side whenever you stop. Don't stop for more than three seconds, as your enthusiastic dog will really feel that it's an eternity!

Puppies, like children, have notoriously short attention spans, so don't overdo it with any of the training. Keep each lesson short. Break it up with a quick run around the yard or a ball toss, repeat the lesson and quit as soon as the pup gets it right. That way, you will always end with a "Good dog."

Life isn't perfect and neither are puppies. A time will come, often around ten months of age, when he'll become "selectively deaf" or choose to "forget" his name. He may respond by wagging his tail (and even seeming to smile at you) with a look that says "Make me!" Laugh, throw his favorite toy and skip the lesson you had planned. Pups will be pups!

THE HEEL EXERCISE
The second most important command to teach, after the come, is the heel. When you are walking your growing puppy, you need to be in control. Besides, it looks terrible to be pulled and yanked down the street, and it's not much fun either. Your eight- to ten-week-old puppy will probably follow you everywhere, but that's his natural instinct, not your control over the situation. However, any time he does follow you, you can say "Heel" and be ahead of the game, as he will learn to associate this command with the

action of following you before you even begin teaching him to heel.

There is a very precise, almost military, procedure for teaching your dog to heel. As with all other obedience training, begin with the dog on your left side. He will be in a very nice sit and you will have the training leash across your chest. Hold the loop and folded leash in your right hand. Pick up the slack leash above the dog in your left hand and hold it loosely at your side. Step out on your left foot as you say "Heel." If the puppy does not move, give a gentle tug or pat your left leg to get him started. If he surges ahead of you, stop and pull him back gently until he is at your side. Tell him to sit and begin again.

Walk a few steps and stop while the puppy is correctly beside you. Tell him to sit and give mild verbal praise. (More enthusiastic praise will encourage him to think the lesson is over.) Repeat the lesson, increasing the number of steps you take only as long as the dog is heeling nicely beside you. When you end the lesson, have him hold the sit, then give him the "Okay" to let him know that this is the end of the lesson. Praise him so that he knows he did a good job.

The cure for excessive pulling (a common problem) is to stop when the dog is no more than 2 or 3 feet ahead of you. Guide him back into position and begin again. With a really determined puller, try switching to a head collar. This will automatically turn the pup's head toward you so you can bring him back easily to the heel position. Give quiet, reassuring praise every time the leash goes slack and he's staying with you.

Staying and heeling can take a lot out of a dog, so provide playtime and free-running exercise to shake off the stress when the lessons are over. You don't want him to associate training with all work and no fun.

TAPERING OFF TIDBITS
Your dog has been watching you—and the hand that treats—throughout all of his lessons, and now it's time to break the treat habit. Begin by giving him treats at the end of each lesson only.

As you make progress in training your Ibizan, give food treats less and praise more to reward your well-behaved dog.

Owning such a handsome breed, it might be fun and rewarding to try showing your Ibizan Hound.

While obedience will probably not be his activity of choice, your Ibizan will comply if he sees that it pleases his beloved master.

your dog along with a qualified instructor and other handlers who may have more dog experience than you is another plus of the class environment. The instructor and other handlers can help you to find the most efficient way of teaching your dog a command or exercise. It's often easier to learn from other people's mistakes than your own. You will also learn all of the requirements for competitive obedience trials, in which you can earn titles and go on to advanced jumping and retrieving exercises, which are fun for many dogs. Obedience classes build the foundation needed for many other canine activities (in which we humans are allowed to participate, too!).

Then start to give a treat after the end of only some of the lessons. At the end of every lesson, as well as during the lessons, be consistent with the praise. Your pup now doesn't know whether he'll get a treat or not, but he should keep performing well just in case! Finally, you will stop giving treat rewards entirely. Save them for something brand-new that you want to teach him. Keep up the praise and you'll always have a "good dog."

OBEDIENCE CLASSES
The advantages of an obedience class are that your dog will have to learn amid the distractions of other people and dogs and that your mistakes will be quickly corrected by the trainer. Teaching

TRAINING FOR OTHER ACTIVITIES

Once your dog has basic obedience under his collar and is 12 months of age, you can enter the world of agility training. Dogs think agility is pure fun, like being turned loose in an amusement park full of obstacles! In addition to agility, there are hunting activities for sporting dogs, lure-coursing events for sighthounds, go-to-ground events for terriers, racing for the Nordic sled dogs, herding trials for the shepherd breeds and tracking, which is open to all "nosey" dogs (which would include all dogs!). For those who like to volunteer, there is the wonderful feeling of owning a therapy dog and visiting

There are some commands that will be less stressful for all parties. Teaching your dog to "shake hands" will be great fun.

hospices, nursing homes and veterans' homes to bring smiles, comfort and companionship to those who live there.

Around the house, your Ibizan Hound can be taught to do some simple chores. You might teach him to carry a basket of household items or to fetch the morning newspaper. The kids can teach the dog all kinds of tricks, from playing hide-and-seek to balancing a biscuit on his nose. A family dog is what rounds out the family. Everything he does, including sitting in your lap or gazing lovingly at you, represents the bonus of owning a dog.

Dog ownership opens up a world of new experiences for dog and owner. Contact a local kennel club to learn about the different activities in which you and your Ibizan can become involved.

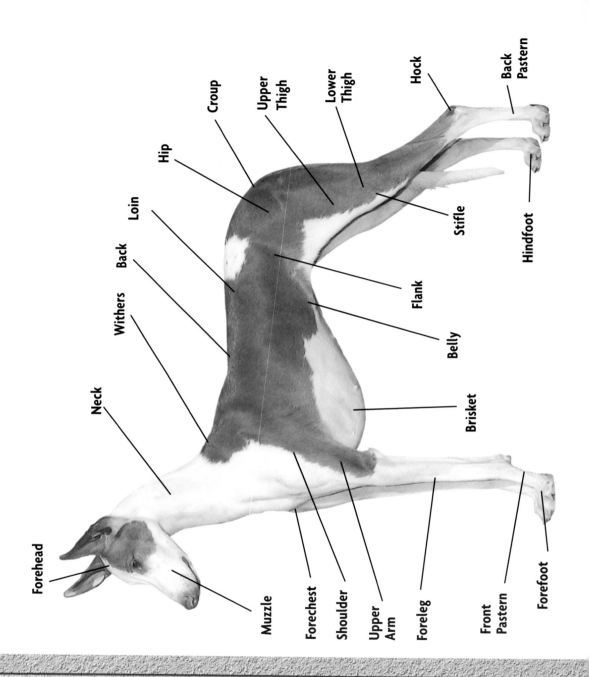

Forehead

Neck

Withers

Back

Loin

Hip

Croup

Upper Thigh

Lower Thigh

Hock

Back Pastern

Stifle

Hindfoot

Flank

Belly

Brisket

Muzzle

Forechest

Shoulder

Upper Arm

Foreleg

Front Pastern

Forefoot

PHYSICAL STRUCTURE OF THE IBIZAN HOUND

HEALTHCARE OF YOUR

IBIZAN HOUND

By Lowell Ackerman DVM, DACVD

HEALTHCARE FOR A LIFETIME

When you own a dog, you become his healthcare advocate over his entire lifespan, as well as being the one to shoulder the financial burden of such care. Accordingly, it is worthwhile to focus on prevention rather than treatment, as you and your pet will both be happier.

Of course, the best place to have begun your program of preventive healthcare is with the initial purchase or adoption of your dog. There is no way of guaranteeing that your new furry friend is free of medical problems, but there are some things you can do to improve your odds. You certainly should have done adequate research into the Ibizan Hound and have selected your puppy carefully rather than buying on impulse. Health issues aside, a large number of pet abandonment and relinquishment cases arise from a mismatch between pet needs and owner expectations. This is entirely preventable with appropriate planning and finding a good breeder.

Regarding healthcare issues specifically, it is very difficult to make blanket statements about where to acquire a problem-free pet, but, again, a reputable breeder is your best bet. In an ideal situation you have the opportunity to see both parents, get references from other owners of the breeder's pups and see genetic-testing documentation for several generations of the litter's ancestors. At the very least, you must thoroughly investigate the Ibizan Hound and the problems inherent in that breed, as well as the genetic testing available to screen for those problems. Genetic testing offers some important benefits, but testing is available for only a few disorders in a relatively small number of breeds and is not available for some of the most common genetic diseases, such as hip dysplasia, cataracts, epilepsy, cardiomyopathy, etc. This area of research is indeed exciting and increasingly important, and advances will continue to be made each year. In fact, recent research has shown that there is an equivalent dog gene for 75% of known human genes, so research done in either species is likely to benefit the other.

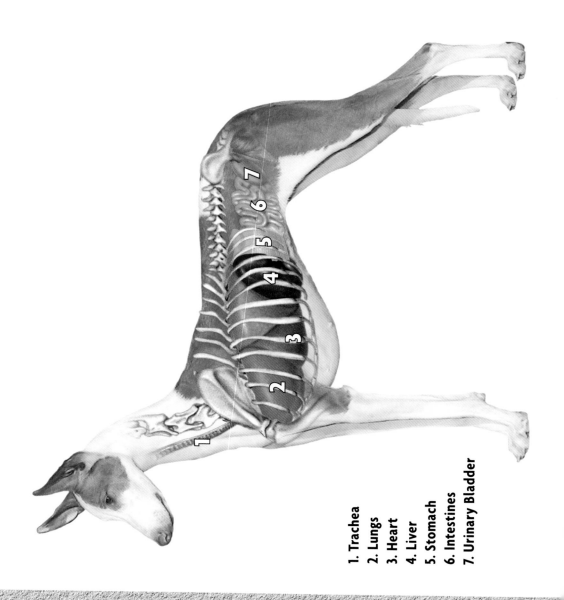

1. Trachea
2. Lungs
3. Heart
4. Liver
5. Stomach
6. Intestines
7. Urinary Bladder

INTERNAL ORGANS OF THE IBIZAN HOUND

We've also discussed that evaluating the behavioral nature of your Ibizan and that of his immediate family members is an important part of the selection process that cannot be underestimated or overemphasized. It is sometimes difficult to evaluate temperament in puppies because certain behavioral tendencies, such as some forms of aggression, may not be immediately evident. More dogs are euthanized each year for behavioral reasons than for all medical conditions combined, so it is critical to take temperament issues seriously. Start with a well-balanced, friendly companion and put the time and effort into proper socialization, and you will both be rewarded with a lifelong valued relationship.

Assuming that you have started off with a pup from healthy, sound stock, you then become responsible for helping your veterinarian keep your pet healthy. Some crucial things happen before you even bring your puppy home. Parasite control typically begins at two weeks of age, and vaccinations typically begin at six to eight weeks of age. A pre-pubertal evaluation is typically scheduled for about six months of age. At this time, a dental evaluation is done (since the adult teeth are now in), heartworm prevention is started and neutering or spaying is most commonly done.

It is critical to commence regular dental care at home if you

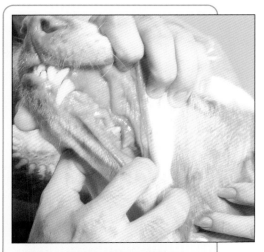

DENTAL WARNING SIGNS

A veterinary dental exam is necessary if you notice one or any combination of the following in your dog:

- Broken, loose or missing teeth
- Loss of appetite (which could be due to mouth pain or illness caused by infection)
- Gum abnormalities, including redness, swelling and bleeding
- Drooling, with or without blood
- Yellowing of the teeth or gumline, indicating tartar
- Bad breath

have not already done so. It may not sound very important, but most dogs have active periodontal disease by four years of age if they don't have their teeth cleaned regularly at home, not just at their veterinary exams. Dental problems lead to more than just bad "doggy breath." Gum disease can have very serious

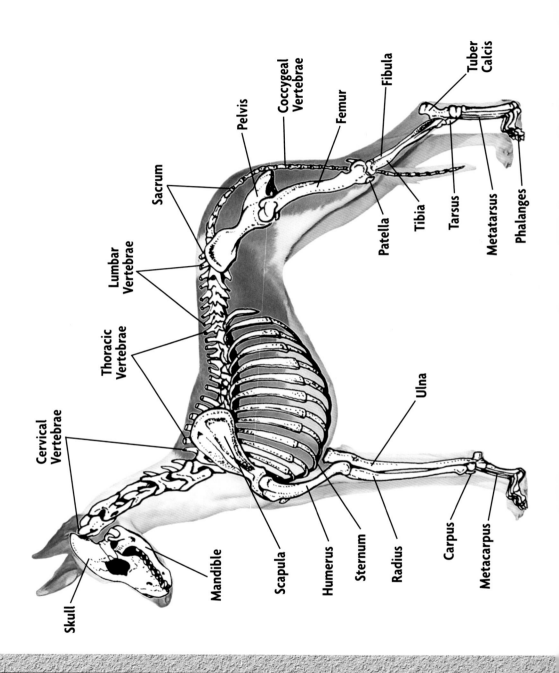

Coccygeal
Vertebrae

Pelvis

Femur

Fibula

Tuber
Calcis

Sacrum

Patella

Tibia

Tarsus

Metatarsus

Phalanges

Lumbar
Vertebrae

Thoracic
Vertebrae

Ulna

Cervical
Vertebrae

Mandible

Scapula

Humerus

Sternum

Radius

Carpus

Metacarpus

Skull

SKELETAL STRUCTURE OF THE IBIZAN HOUND

medical consequences. If you start brushing your dog's teeth and using antiseptic rinses from a young age, your dog will be accustomed to it and will not resist. The results will be healthy dentition, which your pet will need to enjoy a long, healthy life.

Most dogs are considered adults at a year of age, although some larger breeds still have some filling out to do up to about two or so years old. Even individual dogs within each breed have different healthcare requirements, so work with your veterinarian to determine what will be needed and what your role should be. This doctor-client relationship is important, because as vaccination guidelines change, there may not be an annual "vaccine visit" scheduled. You must make sure that you see your veterinarian at least annually, even if no vaccines are due, because this is the best opportunity to coordinate healthcare activities and to make sure that no medical issues creep by unaddressed.

When your Ibizan Hound reaches three-quarters of his anticipated lifespan, he is considered a "senior" and likely requires some special care. In general, if you've been taking great care of your canine companion throughout his formative and adult years, the transition to senior status should be a smooth one. Age is not a disease, and as long as everything is functioning as it should, there is no reason why most of late adulthood should not be rewarding for both you and your pet. This is especially true if you have tended to the details, such as regular veterinary visits, proper dental care, excellent nutrition and management of bone and joint issues.

At this stage in your Ibizan hound's life, your veterinarian may want to schedule visits twice yearly, instead of once, to run some laboratory screenings, electrocardiograms and the like, and to change the diet

TAKING YOUR DOG'S TEMPERATURE

It is important to know how to take your dog's temperature at times when you think he may be ill. It's not the most enjoyable task, but it can be done without too much difficulty. It's easier with a helper, preferably someone with whom the dog is friendly, so that one of you can hold the dog while the other inserts the thermometer.

Before inserting the thermometer, coat the end with petroleum jelly. Insert the thermometer slowly and gently into the dog's rectum about 1 inch. Wait for the reading, about two minutes. Be sure to remove the thermometer carefully and clean it thoroughly after each use.

A dog's normal body temperature is between 100.5 and 102.5 degrees F. Immediate veterinary attention is required if the dog's temperature is below 99 or above 104 degrees F.

to something more digestible. Catching problems early is the best way to manage them effectively. Treating the early stages of heart disease is so much easier than trying to intervene when there is more significant damage to the heart muscle. Similarly, managing the beginning of kidney problems is fairly routine if there is no significant kidney damage. Other problems, like cognitive dysfunction (similar to senility and Alzheimer's disease), cancer, diabetes and arthritis, are more common in older dogs, but all can be treated to help the dog live as many happy, comfortable years as possible. Just as in people, medical management is more effective (and less expensive) when you catch things early.

SELECTING A VETERINARIAN

There is probably no more important decision that you will make regarding your pet's healthcare than the selection of his doctor. Your pet's veterinarian will be a pediatrician, family-practice physician and gerontologist, depending on the dog's life stage, and will be the individual who makes recommendations regarding issues such as when specialists need to be consulted, when diagnostic testing and/or therapeutic intervention is needed and when you will need to seek outside emergency and critical-care services. Your vet will act as your advocate and liaison throughout these processes.

Everyone has his own idea about what to look for in a vet, an individual who will play a big role in his dog's (and, of course, his own) life for many years to come. For some, it is the compassionate caregiver with whom they hope to develop a professional relationship to span the lifetime of their dogs and even their future pets. For others, they are seeking a clinician with keen diagnostic and therapeutic insight who can deliver state-of-the-art healthcare. Still others need a veterinary facility that is open evenings and weekends, is in close proximity or provides mobile veterinary services, to accommodate their schedules; these people may not

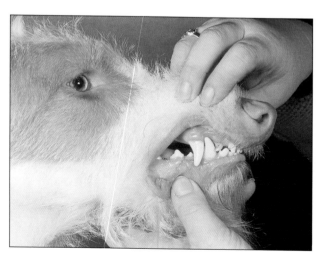

Annual visits to the veterinarian for check-ups will assure that your Ibizan Hound remains in good health.

much mind that their dogs might see different veterinarians on each visit. Just as we have different reasons for selecting our own healthcare professionals (e.g., covered by insurance plan, expert in field, convenient location, etc.), we should not expect that there is a one-size-fits-all recommendation for selecting a veterinarian and veterinary practice. The best advice is to be honest in your assessment of what you expect from a veterinary practice and to conscientiously research the options in your area. You will quickly appreciate that not all veterinary practices are the same, and you will be happiest with one that truly meets your needs.

There is another point to be considered in the selection of veterinary services. Not that long ago, a single veterinarian would attempt to manage all medical and surgical issues as they arose. That was often problematic, because veterinarians are trained in many species and many diseases, and it was just impossible for general veterinary practitioners to be experts in every species, every breed, every field and every ailment. However, just as in the human healthcare fields, specialization has allowed general practitioners to concentrate on primary healthcare delivery, especially wellness and the prevention of infectious diseases, and to utilize a network of specialists to assist in the management of conditions that require specific

expertise and experience. Thus there are now many types of veterinary specialists, including dermatologists, cardiologists, ophthalmologists, surgeons, internists, oncologists, neurologists, behaviorists, criticalists and others to help primary-care veterinarians deal with complicated medical challenges. In most cases, specialists see cases referred by primary-care veterinarians, make diagnoses and set up management plans. From there, the animals' ongoing care is returned to their primary-care veterinarians. This important team approach to your pet's medical-care needs has provided opportunities for advanced care and an unparalleled level of quality to be delivered.

With all of the opportunities for your   to receive high-quality veterinary medical care, there is another topic that needs to be addressed at the same time—cost. It's been said that you can have excellent healthcare or inexpensive healthcare, but never both; this is as true in veterinary medicine as it is in human medicine. While veterinary costs are a fraction of what the same services cost in the human healthcare arena, it is still difficult to deal with unanticipated medical costs, especially since they can easily creep into hundreds or even thousands of dollars if specialists or emergency services become involved. However, there are ways of managing these risks. The easiest is to buy pet health insurance and realize that its foremost purpose is not to cover routine healthcare visits but rather to serve as an umbrella for those rainy days when your pet needs medical care and you don't want to worry about whether or not you can afford that care.

Pet insurance policies are very cost-effective (and very inexpensive by human health-insurance standards), but make sure that you buy the policy long before you intend to use it (preferably starting in puppyhood, because coverage will exclude pre-existing conditions) and that you are actually buying an indemnity insurance plan from an insurance company that is regulated by your state or province. Many insurance policy look-alikes are actually discount clubs that are redeemable only at specific locations and for specific services. An indemnity plan covers your pet at almost all veterinary, specialty and emergency practices and is an excellent way to manage your pet's ongoing healthcare needs.

Your veterinarian will provide your Ibizan with good overall healthcare and alert you to any conditions that require specialized care.

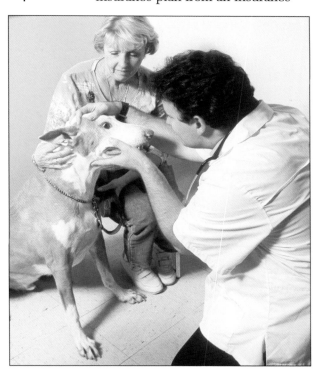

VACCINATIONS AND INFECTIOUS DISEASES

There has never been an easier time to prevent a variety of infectious diseases in your dog, but the advances we've made in veterinary medicine come with a price— choice. Now while it may seem that choice is a good thing (and it is), it has never been more difficult for the pet owner (or the veterinarian) to make an informed decision about the best way to protect pets through vaccination.

Years ago, it was just accepted that puppies got a starter series of vaccinations and then annual "boosters" throughout their lives to keep them protected. As more and more vaccines became available, consumers wanted the convenience of having all of that protection in a single injection. The result was "multivalent" vaccines that crammed a lot of protection into a single syringe. The manufacturers' recommendations were to give the vaccines annually, and this was a simple enough protocol to follow.

COMMON INFECTIOUS DISEASES

Let's discuss some of the diseases that create the need for vaccination in the first place. Following are the major canine infectious diseases and a simple explanation of each.

Rabies: A devastating viral disease that can be fatal in dogs and people. In fact, vaccination of dogs and cats is an important public-health measure to create a resistant animal buffer population to protect people from contracting the disease. Vaccination schedules are determined on a government level and are not optional for pet owners; rabies vaccination is required by law in all 50 states.

Parvovirus: A severe, potentially life-threatening disease that is easily transmitted between dogs. There are four strains of the virus, but it is believed that there is significant "cross-protection" between strains that may be included in individual vaccines.

Distemper: A potentially severe and life-threatening disease with a relatively high risk of exposure, especially in certain regions. In very high-risk distemper environments, young pups may be vaccinated with human measles vaccine, a related virus that offers cross-protection when administered at four to ten weeks of age.

Hepatitis: Caused by canine adenovirus type 1 (CAV-1), but since vaccination with the causative virus has a higher rate of adverse effects, cross-protection is derived from the use of adenovirus type 2 (CAV-2), a cause of respiratory disease and one of the potential causes of canine cough. Vaccination with CAV-2 provides long-term immunity against hepatitis, but relatively less protection against respiratory infection.

Canine cough: Also called tracheobronchitis, actually a fairly complicated result of viral and bacterial offenders; therefore, even with vaccination, protection is incomplete. Wherever dogs congregate, canine cough will likely be spread among them. Intranasal vaccination with *Bordetella* and parainfluenza is the best safeguard, but the duration of immunity does not appear to be very long, typically a year at most. These are non-core vaccines, but vaccination is sometimes mandated by boarding kennels, obedience classes, dog shows and other places where dogs congregate to try to minimize spread of infection.

Leptospirosis: A potentially fatal disease that is more common in some geographic regions. It is capable of being spread to humans. The disease varies with the individual "serovar," or strain, of *Leptospira* involved. Since there does not appear to be much cross-protection between serovars, protection is only as good as the likelihood that the serovar in the vaccine is the same as the one in the pet's local environment. Problems with *Leptospira* vaccines are that protection does not last very long, side effects are not uncommon and a large percentage of dogs (perhaps 30%) may not respond to vaccination.

Borrelia burgdorferi: The cause of Lyme disease, the risk of which varies with the geographic area in which the pet lives and travels. Lyme disease is spread by deer ticks in the eastern US and western black-legged ticks in the western part of the country, and the risk of exposure is high in some regions. Lameness, fever and inappetence are most commonly seen in affected dogs. The extent of protection from the vaccine has not been conclusively demonstrated.

Coronavirus: This disease has a high risk of exposure, especially in areas where dogs congregate, but it typically causes only mild to moderate digestive upset (diarrhea, vomiting, etc.). Vaccines are available, but the duration of protection is believed to be relatively short and the effectiveness of the vaccine in preventing infection is considered low.

There are many other vaccinations available, including those for *Giardia* and canine adenovirus-1. While there may be some specific indications for their use, and local risk factors to be considered, they are not widely recommended for most dogs.

SPAY'S THE WAY

Although spaying a female dog qualifies as major surgery—an ovariohysterectomy, in fact—this procedure is regarded as routine when performed by a qualified veterinarian on a healthy dog. The advantages to spaying a bitch are many and great. Spayed dogs do not develop uterine cancer or any life-threatening diseases of the genitals. Likewise, spayed dogs are at a significantly reduced risk of breast cancer. Bitches (and owners) are relieved of the demands of heat cycles. A spayed bitch will not leave bloody stains on your furniture during estrus, and you will not have to contend with single-minded macho males trying to climb your fence in order to seduce her. The spayed bitch's coat will not show the ill effects of her estrogen level's climbing such as a dull, lackluster outer coat or patches of hairlessness.

However, as veterinary medicine has become more sophisticated and we have started looking more at healthcare quandaries rather than convenience, it became necessary to reevaluate the situation and deal with some tough questions. It is important to realize that whether or not to use a particular vaccine depends on the risk of contracting the disease against which it protects, the severity of the disease if it is contracted, the duration of immunity provided by the vaccine, the safety of the product and the needs of the individual animal. In a very general sense, rabies, distemper, hepatitis and parvovirus are considered core vaccine needs, while parainfluenza, *Bordetella bronchiseptica*, leptospirosis, coronavirus and borreliosis (Lyme disease) are considered non-core needs and best reserved for animals that demonstrate reasonable risk of contracting the diseases.

NEUTERING/SPAYING

Sterilization procedures (neutering for males/spaying for females) are meant to accomplish several purposes. While the underlying premise is to address the risk of pet overpopulation, there are also some medical and behavioral benefits to the surgeries as well. For females, spaying prior to the first estrus (heat cycle) leads to a marked reduction in the risk of mammary cancer. There also will be no manifestations of "heat" to attract male dogs and no bleeding in the house. For males, there is prevention of testicular cancer and a reduction in the risk of prostate problems. In both sexes there may be some limited reduction in aggressive behaviors toward other dogs, and some diminishing of urine marking, roaming and mounting.

While neutering and spaying do indeed prevent animals from

contributing to pet overpopulation, even no-cost and low-cost neutering options have not eliminated the problem. Perhaps one of the main reasons for this is that individuals that intentionally breed their dogs and those that allow their animals to run at large are the main causes of unwanted offspring. Also, animals in shelters are often there because they were abandoned or relinquished, not because they came from unplanned matings. Neutering/ spaying is important, but it should be considered in the context of the real causes of animals' ending up in shelters and eventually being euthanized.

One of the important consider-ations regarding neutering is that it is a surgical procedure. This sometimes gets lost in discussions of low-cost procedures and commoditization of the process. In females, spaying is specifically referred to as an ovariohysterec-tomy. In this procedure, a midline incision is made in the abdomen and the entire uterus and both ovaries are surgically removed. While this is a major invasive surgical procedure, it usually has few complications, because it is typically performed on healthy young animals. However, it is major surgery, as any woman who has had a hysterectomy will attest.

In males, neutering has traditionally referred to castration, which involves the surgical removal of both testicles. While still a significant piece of surgery, there is not the abdominal exposure that is required in the female surgery. In addition, there is now a chemical sterilization option, in which a solution is injected into each testicle, leading to atrophy of the sperm-producing cells. This can typically be done under sedation rather than full anesthesia. This is a relatively new approach, and there are no long-term clinical studies yet available.

Neutering/spaying is typically done around six months of age at most veterinary hospitals, although techniques have been pioneered to perform the procedures in animals as young as eight weeks of age. In general, the surgeries on the very young animals are done for the specific reason of sterilizing them before they go to their new homes. This is done in some shelter hospitals for assurance that the animals will definitely not produce any pups. Otherwise, these organizations need to rely on owners to comply with their wishes to have the animals "altered" at a later date, something that does not always happen.

There are some exciting immunocontraceptive "vaccines" currently under development, and there may be a time when contra-ception in pets will not require surgical procedures.

S. E. M. BY DR. DENNIS KUNKEL, UNIVERSITY OF HAWAII

A scanning electron micrograph of a dog flea, *Ctenocephalides canis,* on dog hair.

EXTERNAL PARASITES

FLEAS

Fleas have been around for millions of years and, while we have better tools now for controlling them than at any time in the past, there still is little chance that they will end up on an endangered species list. Actually, they are very well adapted to living on our pets, and they continue to adapt as we make advances.

The female flea can consume 15 times her weight in blood during active reproduction and can lay as many as 40 eggs a day. These eggs are very resistant to the effects of insecticides. They hatch into larvae, which then mature and spin cocoons. The immature fleas reside in this pupal stage until the time is right for feeding. This pupal stage is also very resistant to the effects of insecticides, and pupae can last in the environment without feeding for many months. Newly emergent fleas are attracted to animals by the warmth of the animals' bodies, movement and exhaled carbon dioxide. However, when they first emerge from their cocoons, they orient towards light; thus when an animal passes between a flea and the light source, casting a shadow, the flea pounces and starts to feed. If the animal turns out to be a dog or cat, the reproductive cycle continues. If the flea lands on another type of animal, including a

FLEA PREVENTION FOR YOUR DOG

- Discuss with your veterinarian the safest product to protect your dog, likely in the form of a monthly tablet or a liquid preparation placed on the back of the dog's neck.
- For dogs suffering from flea-bite dermatitis, a shampoo or topical insecticide treatment is required.
- Your lawn and property should be sprayed with an insecticide designed to kill fleas and ticks that lurk outdoors.
- Using a flea comb, check the dog's coat regularly for any signs of parasites.
- Practice good housekeeping. Vacuum floors, carpets and furniture regularly, especially in the areas that the dog frequents, and wash the dog's bedding weekly.
- Follow up house-cleaning with carpet shampoos and sprays to rid the house of fleas at all stages of development. Insect growth regulators are the safest option.

person, the flea will bite but will then look for a more appropriate host. An emerging adult flea can survive without feeding for up to 12 months but, once it tastes blood, it can survive off its host for only 3 to 4 days.

It was once thought that fleas spend most of their lives in the environment, but we now know that fleas won't willingly jump off a dog unless leaping to another dog or when physically removed by brushing, bathing or other manipulation. Flea eggs, on the other hand, are shiny and smooth, and they roll off the animal and into the environment. The eggs, larvae and pupae then exist in the environment, but once the adult finds a susceptible animal, it's home sweet home until the flea is forced to seek refuge elsewhere.

Since adult fleas live on the animal and immature forms survive in the environment, a successful treatment plan must address all stages of the flea life cycle. There are now several safe and effective flea-control products that can be applied on a monthly basis. These include fipronil, imidacloprid, selamectin and permethrin (found in several formulations). Most of these products have significant flea-killing rates within 24 hours. However, none of them will control the immature forms in the environment. To accomplish this, there are a variety of insect growth regulators that can be sprayed into the

THE FLEA'S LIFE CYCLE

What came first, the flea or the egg? This age-old mystery is more difficult to comprehend than the actual cycle of the flea. Fleas usually live only about four months. A female can lay 2,000 eggs in her lifetime.

Egg

Larva

After ten days of rolling around your carpet or under your furniture, the eggs hatch into larvae, which feed on various and sundry debris. In days or months, depending on the climate, the larvae spin cocoons and develop into the pupal or nymph stage, which quickly develop into fleas.

Pupa

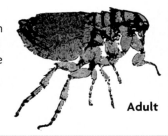
Adult

These immature fleas must locate a host within 10 to 14 days or they will die. Only about 1% of the flea population exist as adult fleas, while the other 99% exist as eggs, larvae or pupae.

environment (e.g., pyriproxyfen, methoprene, fenoxycarb) as well as insect development inhibitors such as lufenuron that can be administered. These compounds have no effect on adult fleas, but they stop immature forms from developing into adults. In years gone by, we relied heavily on toxic insecticides (such as organophosphates, organochlorines and carbamates) to manage the flea problem, but today's options are not only much safer to use on our pets but also safer for the environment.

TICKS

Ticks are members of the spider class (arachnids) and are blood-sucking parasites capable of transmitting a variety of diseases, including Lyme disease, ehrlichiosis, babesiosis and Rocky Mountain spotted fever. It's easy to see ticks on your own skin, but it is more of a challenge when your furry companion is affected. Whenever you happen to be planning a stroll in a tick-infested area (especially forests, grassy or wooded areas or parks) be prepared to do a thorough inspection of your dog afterward to search for ticks. Ticks can be tricky,

> **TICK CONTROL**
> Removal of underbrush and leaf litter and the thinning of trees in areas where tick control is desired are recommended. These actions remove the cover and food sources for small animals that serve as hosts for ticks. With continued mowing of grasses in these areas, the probability of ticks' surviving is further reduced. A variety of insecticide ingredients (e.g., resmethrin, carbaryl, permethrin, chlorpyrifos, dioxathion and allethrin) are registered for tick control around the home.

so make sure you spend time looking in the ears, between the toes and everywhere else where a tick might hide. Ticks need to be attached for 24–72 hours before they transmit most of the diseases that they carry, so you do have a window of opportunity for some preventive intervention.

Female ticks live to eat and breed. They can lay between 4,000 and 5,000 eggs and they die soon after. Males, on the other hand, live only to mate with the females and continue the process as long as they are able. Most ticks live on multiple hosts before parasitizing dogs. The immature forms typically reside on grass and shrubs, waiting for susceptible animals to walk by. The larvae and nymph stages typically feed on wildlife.

If only a few ticks are present on a dog, they can be plucked out, but it is important to remove the

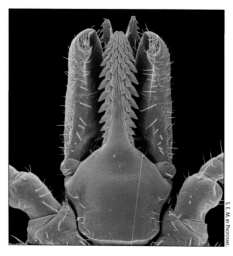

A scanning electron micrograph of the head of a female deer tick, *Ixodes dammini*, a parasitic tick that carries Lyme disease.

S.E.M. BY PHOTOTAKE

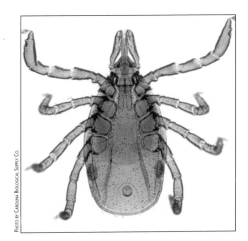

Photo by Carolina Biological Supply Co.

diseases caused by mites are referred to as "mange," and there are many different forms seen in dogs. These forms are very different from one another, each one warranting an individual description.

Sarcoptic mange, or scabies, is one of the itchiest conditions that affects dogs. The microscopic *Sarcoptes* mites burrow into the superficial layers of the skin and can drive dogs crazy with itchiness. They are also communicable to people, although they can't complete their reproductive cycle on people. In addition to being tiny, the mites also are often difficult to find when trying to make a diagnosis. Skin scrapings from multiple areas are examined microscopically but, even then, sometimes the mites cannot be found.

Deer tick,
Ixodes dammini.

entire head and mouthparts, which may be deeply embedded in the skin. This is best accomplished with forceps designed especially for this purpose; fingers can be used but should be protected with rubber gloves, plastic wrap or at least a paper towel. The tick should be grasped as closely as possible to the animal's skin and should be pulled upward with steady, even pressure. Do not squeeze, crush or puncture the body of the tick or you risk exposure to any disease carried by that tick. Once the ticks have been removed, the sites of attachment should be disinfected. Your hands should then be washed with soap and water to further minimize risk of contagion. The tick should be disposed of in a container of alcohol or household bleach.

MITES
Mites are tiny arachnid parasites that parasitize the skin of dogs. Skin

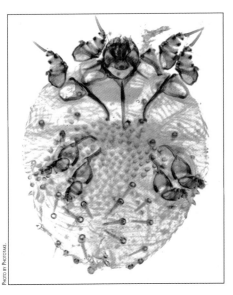

Photo by Phototake.

**Sarcoptes scabiei,
commonly known
as the "itch mite."**

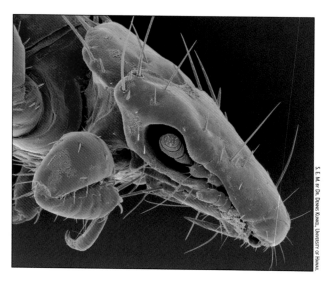

S.E.M. BY DR. DENNIS KUNKEL, UNIVERSITY OF HAWAII

Micrograph of a dog louse, *Heterodoxus spiniger*. Female lice attach their eggs to the hairs of the dog. As the eggs hatch, the larval lice bite and feed on the blood. Lice can also feed on dead skin and hair. This feeding activity can cause hair loss and skin problems.

Illustration of *Demodex folliculoram*.

Fortunately, scabies is relatively easy to treat, and there are a variety of products that will successfully kill the mites. Since the mites can't live in the environment for very long without feeding, a complete cure is usually possible within four to eight weeks.

Cheyletiellosis is caused by a relatively large mite, which sometimes can be seen even without a microscope. Often referred to as "walking dandruff," this also causes itching, but not usually as profound as with scabies. While *Cheyletiella* mites can survive somewhat longer in the environment than scabies mites, they too are relatively easy to treat, being responsive to not only the medications used to treat scabies but also often to flea-control products.

Otodectes cynotis is the canine ear mite and is one of the more common causes of mange, especially in young dogs in shelters or pet stores. That's because the mites are typically present in large numbers and are quickly spread to nearby animals. The mites rarely do much harm but can be difficult to eradicate if the treatment regimen is not comprehensive. While many try to treat the condition with ear drops only, this is the most common cause of treatment failure. Ear drops cause the mites to simply move out of the ears and as far away as possible (usually to the base of the tail) until the insecticide levels in the ears drop to an acceptable level—then it's back to business as usual! The successful treatment of ear mites requires treating all animals in the household with a systemic insecticide, such as selamectin, or a combination of miticidal ear drops combined with whole-body flea-control preparations.

Demodicosis, sometimes referred to as red mange, can be one of the most difficult forms of mange to treat. Part of the problem has to do with the fact that the mites live in the hair follicles and they are relatively well shielded from topical and systemic products. The main issue, however, is that demodectic mange typically results only when there is some underlying process interfering with the dog's immune system.

ILLUSTRATION BY PHOTOTAKE

Since *Demodex* mites are normal residents of the skin of mammals, including humans, there is usually a mite population explosion only when the immune system fails to keep the number of mites in check. In young animals, the immune deficit may be transient or may reflect an actual inherited immune problem. In older animals, demodicosis is usually seen only when there is another disease hampering the immune system, such as diabetes, cancer, thyroid problems or the use of immune-suppressing drugs. Accordingly, treatment involves not only trying to kill the mange mites but also discerning what is interfering with immune function and correcting it if possible.

Chiggers represent several different species of mite that don't parasitize dogs specifically, but do latch on to passersby and can cause irritation. The problem is most prevalent in wooded areas in the late summer and fall. Treatment is not difficult, as the mites do not complete their life cycle on dogs and are susceptible to a variety of miticidal products.

MOSQUITOES

Mosquitoes have long been known to transmit a variety of diseases to people, as well as just being biting pests during warm weather. They also pose a real risk to pets. Not only do they carry deadly heart-worms but recently there also has been much concern over their involvement with West Nile virus. While we can avoid heartworm with the use of preventive medications, there are no such preventives for West Nile virus. The only method of prevention in endemic areas is active mosquito control. Fortunately, most dogs that have been exposed to the virus only developed flu-like symptoms and, to date, there have not been the large number of reported deaths in canines as seen in some other species.

MOSQUITO REPELLENT

Low concentrations of DEET (less than 10%), found in many human mosquito repellents, have been safely used in dogs but, in these concentrations, probably give only about two hours of protection. DEET may be safe in these small concentrations, but since it is not licensed for use on dogs, there is no research proving its safety for dogs. Products containing permethrin give the longest-lasting protection, perhaps two to four weeks. As DEET is not licensed for use on dogs, and both DEET and permethrin can be quite toxic to cats, appropriate care should be exercised. Other products, such as those containing oil of citronella, also have some mosquito-repellent activity, but typically have a relatively short duration of action.

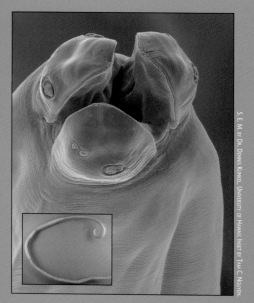

The ascarid roundworm *Toxocara canis*, showing the mouth with three lips. INSET: Photomicrograph of the roundworm *Ascaris lumbricoides*.

The hookworm *Ancylostoma caninum* infests the intestines of dogs. INSET: Note the row of hooks at the posterior end, used to anchor the worm to the intestinal wall.

S. E. M. BY DR. DENNIS KUNKEL, UNIVERSITY OF HAWAII. INSET BY TAM C. NGUYEN.

S. E. M. BY DR. DENNIS KUNKEL, UNIVERSITY OF HAWAII.

INTERNAL PARASITES: WORMS

ASCARIDS

Ascarids are intestinal roundworms that rarely cause severe disease in dogs. Nonetheless, they are of major public health significance because they can be transferred to people. Sadly, it is children who are most commonly affected by the parasite, probably from inadvertently ingesting ascarid-contaminated soil. In fact, many yards and children's sandboxes contain appreciable numbers of ascarid eggs. So, while ascarids don't bite dogs or latch onto their intestines to suck blood, they do cause some nasty medical conditions in children and are best eradicated from our furry friends. Because pups can start passing ascarid eggs by three weeks of age, most parasite-control programs begin at two weeks of age and are repeated every two weeks until pups are eight weeks old. It is important to realize that bitches can pass ascarids to their pups even if they test negative prior to whelping. Accordingly, bitches are best treated at the same time as the pups.

HOOKWORMS

Unlike ascarids, hookworms do latch onto a dog's intestinal tract and can cause significant loss of blood and protein. Similar to ascarids, hookworms can be transmitted to humans, where they cause a condition known as cutaneous larval migrans. Dogs can become infected either by consuming the infective larvae or by the larvae's penetrating the skin directly. People most often get infected when they are lying on the ground (such as on a beach) and the larvae penetrate the skin. Yes, the larvae can penetrate through a beach blanket. Hookworms are typically susceptible to the same medications used to treat ascarids.

HEARTWORMS

Heartworm disease is caused by the parasite *Dirofilaria immitis* and is seen in dogs around the world. A member of the roundworm group, it is spread between dogs by the bite of an infected mosquito. The

WORM-CONTROL GUIDELINES

- Practice sanitary habits with your dog and home.
- Clean up after your dog and don't let him sniff or eat other dogs' droppings.
- Control insects and fleas in the dog's environment. Fleas, lice, cockroaches, beetles, mice and rats can act as hosts for various worms.
- Prevent dogs from eating uncooked meat, raw poultry and dead animals.
- Keep dogs and children from playing in sand and soil.
- Kennel dogs on cement or gravel; avoid dirt runs.
- Administer heartworm preventives regularly.
- Have your vet examine your dog's stools at your annual visits.
- Select a boarding kennel carefully so as to avoid contamination from other dogs or an unsanitary environment.
- Prevent dogs from roaming. Obey local leash laws.

Ascarid *Rhabditis*

Hookworm *Ancylostoma caninum*

Tapeworm *Dipylidium caninum*

Heartworm *Dirofilaria immitis*

mosquito injects infective larvae into the dog's skin with its bite, and these larvae develop under the skin for a period of time before making their way to the heart. There they develop into adults, which grow and create blockages of the heart, lungs and major blood vessels there. They also start producing offspring (microfilariae), and these microfilariae circulate in the bloodstream, waiting to hitch a ride when the next mosquito bites. Once in the mosquito, the microfilariae develop into infective larvae and the entire process is repeated.

When dogs get infected with heartworm, over time they tend to develop symptoms associated with heart disease, such as coughing, exercise intolerance and potentially many other manifestations. Diagnosis is confirmed by either seeing the microfilariae themselves in blood samples or using immunologic tests (antigen testing) to identify the presence of adult heartworms. Since antigen tests measure the presence of adult heartworms and microfilarial tests measure offspring produced by adults, neither are positive until six to seven months after the initial infection. However, the beginning of damage can occur by fifth-stage larvae as early as three months after infection. Thus it is possible for dogs to be harboring problem-causing larvae for up to three months before either type of test would identify an infection.

The good news is that there are great protocols available for preventing heartworm in dogs. Testing is critical in the process, and it is important to understand the benefits as well as the limitations of such testing. All dogs six months of age or older that have not been on continuous heartworm-preventive medication should be screened with microfilarial or antigen tests. For dogs receiving preventive medication, periodic antigen testing helps assess the

The dog tapeworm *Taenia pisiformis*.

S. E. M. BY DR. DENNIS KUNKEL, UNIVERSITY OF HAWAII

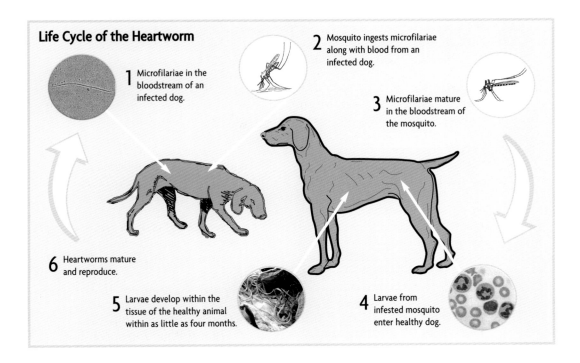

Life Cycle of the Heartworm

1 Microfilariae in the bloodstream of an infected dog.

2 Mosquito ingests microfilariae along with blood from an infected dog.

3 Microfilariae mature in the bloodstream of the mosquito.

6 Heartworms mature and reproduce.

5 Larvae develop within the tissue of the healthy animal within as little as four months.

4 Larvae from infested mosquito enter healthy dog.

effectiveness of the preventives. The American Heartworm Society guidelines suggest that annual retesting may not be necessary when owners have absolutely provided continuous heartworm prevention. Retesting on a two- to three-year interval may be sufficient in these cases. However, your veterinarian will likely have specific guidelines under which heartworm preventives will be prescribed, and many prefer to err on the side of safety and usually retest annually.

It is indeed fortunate that heartworm is relatively easy to prevent, because treatments can be as life-threatening as the disease itself. Treatment requires a two-step process that kills the adult heartworms first and then the microfilariae. Prevention is obviously preferable; this involves a once-monthly oral or topical treatment. The most common oral preventives include ivermectin (not suitable for some breeds), moxidectin and milbemycin oxime; the once-a-month topical drug selamectin provides heartworm protection in addition to flea, some types of tick and other parasite controls.

Is dog showing in your blood? Are you excited by the idea of gaiting your handsome Ibizan Hound around the ring to the thunderous applause of an enthusiastic audience? Are you certain that your beloved Ibizan Hound is flawless? You are not alone! Every loving owner thinks that his dog has no faults, or too few to mention. No matter how many times an owner reads the breed standard, he cannot find any faults in his aristocratic companion dog. If this sounds like you, and if you are considering entering your Ibizan Hound in a dog show, here are some basic questions to ask yourself:

• Did you purchase a "show-quality" puppy from the breeder?
• Is your puppy at least six months of age?
• Does the puppy exhibit correct show type for his breed?
• Does your puppy have any disqualifying faults?

The judge performs a hands-on examination of each dog, feeling for correct body construction and soundness.

- Is your Ibizan Hound registered with the American Kennel Club?
- How much time do you have to devote to training, grooming, conditioning and exhibiting your dog?
- Do you understand the rules and regulations of a dog show?
- Do you have time to learn how to show your dog properly?
- Do you have the financial resources to invest in showing your dog?
- Will you show the dog yourself or hire a professional handler?
- Do you have a vehicle that can accommodate your weekend trips to the dog shows?

FOR MORE INFORMATION...

For reliable up-to-date information about registration, dog shows and other canine competitions, contact one of the national registries by mail or via the Internet.

American Kennel Club
5580 Centerview Dr., Raleigh, NC 27606-3390
www.akc.org

United Kennel Club
100 E. Kilgore Road, Kalamazoo, MI 49002
www.ukcdogs.com

Canadian Kennel Club
89 Skyway Ave., Suite 100, Etobicoke, Ontario
M9W 6R4, Canada
www.ckc.ca

The Kennel Club
1-5 Clarges St., Piccadilly,
London W1Y 8AB, UK
www.the-kennel-club.org.uk

Success in the show ring requires more than a pretty face, a waggy tail and a pocketful of liver. Even though dog shows can be exciting and enjoyable, the sport of conformation makes great demands on the exhibitors and the dogs. Winning exhibitors live for their dogs, devoting time and money to their dogs' presentation, conditioning and training. Very few novices, even those with good dogs, will find themselves in the winners' circle, though it does happen. Don't be disheartened, though. Every exhibitor began as a novice and worked his way up to the Group ring. It's the "working your way up" part that you must keep in mind.

Assuming that you have purchased a puppy of the correct type and quality for showing, let's begin to examine the world of showing and what's required to get started. Although the entry fee into

In the ring, the judge will note how the dog conforms to the ideal set forth in the breed standard, which is what the dog is being compared to, not the other dogs.

While showing isn't without its price, watching your dog be victorious in the ring may certainly be well worth the investment.

a dog show is nominal, there are lots of other hidden costs involved with "finishing" your Ibizan Hound, that is, making him a champion. Things like equipment, travel, training and conditioning all cost money. A more serious campaign will include fees for a professional handler, boarding, cross-country travel and advertising. Top-winning show dogs can represent a very considerable investment—over $100,000 has been spent in campaigning some dogs. (The investment can be less, of course, for owners who don't use professional handlers.)

Many owners, on the other hand, enter their "average" Ibizan Hounds in dog shows for the fun and enjoyment of it. Dog showing makes an absorbing hobby, with many rewards for dogs and owners alike. If you're having fun, meeting other people who share your interests and enjoying the overall experience, you likely will catch the "bug." Once the dog-show bug bites, its effects can last a lifetime; it's certainly much better than a deer tick! Soon you will be envisioning yourself in the center ring at the Westminster Kennel Club Dog Show in New York City, competing for the prestigious Best in Show cup. This magical dog show is televised annually from Madison Square Garden, and the victorious dog becomes a celebrity overnight.

AKC CONFORMATION SHOWING

GETTING STARTED

Visiting a dog show as a spectator is a great place to start. Pick up the show catalog to find out what time your breed is being shown, who is judging the breed and in which ring the classes will be held. To start, Ibizan Hounds compete against other Ibizan Hounds, and the winner is selected as Best of Breed by the judge. This is the procedure for each breed. At a group show, all of the Best of Breed winners go on to compete for Group One (first place) in their respective group. For example, all Best of Breed winners in a given group compete against each other; this is done for all seven groups. Finally, all seven group winners go head to head in the ring for the Best in Show award.

What most spectators don't understand is the basic idea of conformation. A dog show is often referred to as a "conformation"

ON THE MOVE

The truest test of a dog's proper structure is his gait, the way the dog moves. The American Kennel Club defines gait as "the pattern of footsteps at various rates of speed, each pattern distinguished by a particular rhythm and footfall." That the dog moves smoothly and effortlessly indicates to the judge that the dog's structure is well made. From the four-beat gallop, the fastest of canine gaits, to the high-lifting hackney gait, each breed varies in its correct gait; not every breed is expected to move in the same way. Each breed standard defines the correct gait for its breed and often identifies movement faults, such as toeing in, side-winding, over-reaching or crossing over.

A quality handler plays a large role in whether or not a dog will stack up in the show ring.

show. This means that the judge should decide how each dog stacks up (conforms) to the breed standard for his given breed: how well does this Ibizan Hound conform to the ideal representative detailed in the standard? Ideally, this is what happens. In reality, however, this ideal often gets slighted as the judge compares Ibizan Hound #1 to Ibizan Hound #2. Again, the ideal is that each dog is judged based on his merits in comparison to his breed standard, not in comparison to the other dogs in the ring. It is easier for judges to compare dogs of the same breed to decide which they think is the better specimen; in the Group and Best in Show ring, however, it is very difficult to compare one breed to another, like apples to oranges. Thus the dog's conformation to the breed standard—not to mention advertising dollars and good handling—is essential to success in conformation shows. The dog

The Hound Group judging is underway as this handsome Ibizan Hound looks up attentively at his handler.

described in the standard (the standard for each AKC breed is written and approved by the breed's national parent club and then submitted to the AKC for approval) is the perfect dog of that breed, and breeders keep their eyes on the standard when they choose which dogs to breed, hoping to get closer and closer to the ideal with each litter.

Another good first step for the novice is to join a dog club. You will be astonished by the many and different kinds of dog clubs in the country, with about 5,000 clubs holding events every year. Most clubs require that prospective new members present two letters of recommendation from existing members. Perhaps you've made some friends visiting a show held by a particular club and you would like to join that club. Dog clubs may specialize in a single breed, like a local or regional Ibizan Hound club, or in a specific pursuit, such as obedience, tracking or hunting tests. There are all-breed clubs for all-dog enthusiasts; they sponsor special training days, seminars on topics like grooming or handling or lectures on breeding or canine genetics. There are also clubs that specialize in certain types of dogs, like herding dogs, hunting dogs, companion dogs, etc.

A parent club is the national organization, sanctioned by the AKC, which promotes and

MEET THE AKC

The American Kennel Club is the main governing body of the dog sport in the United States. Founded in 1884, the AKC consists of 500 or more independent dog clubs plus 4,500 affiliated clubs, all of which follow the AKC rules and regulations. Additionally, the AKC maintains a registry for pure-bred dogs in the US and works to preserve the integrity of the sport and its continuation in the country. Over 1,000,000 dogs are registered each year, representing about 150 recognized breeds. There are over 15,000 competitive events held annually for which over 2,000,000 dogs enter to participate. Dogs compete to earn over 40 different titles, from champion to Companion Dog to Master Agility Champion.

safeguards its breed in the country. The Ibizan Hound Club of the United States was formed in the mid-1970s and can be contacted on the Internet at www.geocities.com/Heartland/ Pointe/2446/IHCUS.htm. The parent club holds an annual national specialty show, usually in a different city each year, in which many of the country's top dogs, handlers and breeders gather to compete. At a specialty show, only members of a single breed are invited to participate. There are also group specialties, in which all members of a group are invited.

For more information about dog clubs in your area, contact the AKC at www.akc.org on the Internet or write them at their Raleigh, NC address.

HOW SHOWS ARE ORGANIZED

Three kinds of conformation shows are offered by the AKC. There is the all-breed show, in which all AKC-recognized breeds can compete; the specialty show, which is for one breed only and usually sponsored by the breed's parent club; and the group show,

Ch. Serandida's Only at Sunarise, "Riser," was a top contender, Hound Group winner and Best of Breed at Westminster in the late 1980s.

for all breeds in one of the AKC's seven groups. The Ibizan Hound competes in the Hound Group.

For a dog to become an AKC champion of record, the dog must earn 15 points at shows. The points must be awarded by at least three different judges and must include two "majors" under different judges. A "major" is a three-, four- or five-point win, and the number of points per win is determined by the number of dogs competing in the show on that day. (Dogs that are absent or are excused are not counted.) The number of points that are awarded varies from breed to breed. More dogs are needed to attain a major in more popular breeds, and fewer dogs are needed in less popular breeds. Yearly, the AKC evaluates the number of dogs in competition in each division (there are 14

divisions in all, based on geography) and may or may not change the numbers of dogs required for each number of points. The Ibizan Hound attracts numerically proportionate representation at all-breed shows.

Only one dog and one bitch of each breed can win points at a given show. There are no "co-ed" classes except for champions of record. Dogs and bitches do not compete against each other until they are champions. Dogs that are not champions (referred to as "class dogs") compete in one of five classes. The class in which a dog is entered depends on age and previous show wins. First there is the Puppy Class (sometimes divided further into classes for 6- to 9-month-olds and 9- to 12- month-olds); next is the Novice Class (for dogs that have no points toward their championship and whose only first-place wins have come in the Puppy Class or the Novice Class, the latter class limited to three first places); then there is the American-bred Class (for dogs bred in the US); the Bred-by-Exhibitor Class (for dogs handled by their breeders or by immediate family members of their breeders); and the Open Class (for any non-champions). Any dog may enter the Open Class,

Ch. Luxor's Playmate of the Year was Top Hound and one of the top dogs of any breed in 2003. She is shown winning one of her record 39 all-breed Bests in Show that year at Gloucester Kennel Club of Virginia under judge Dr. James Edward, handled by Clint Livingston.

Ch. Gryphon's Stellar Eminence, the top wire-haired Ibizan, is shown winning Best in Show at Hilton Head Island Kennel Club in 2004 under judge Patricia Trotter.

regardless of age or win history, but to be competitive the dog should be older and have ring experience.

The judge at the show begins judging the male dogs in the Puppy Class(es) and proceeds through the other classes. The judge awards first through fourth place in each class. The first-place winners of each class then compete with one another in the Winners Class to determine Winners Dog. The judge then starts over with the bitches, beginning with the Puppy Class(es) and proceeding up to the Winners Class to award Winners Bitch, just as he did with the dogs. A Reserve Winners Dog and Reserve Winners Bitch are also selected; they could be awarded the points in the case of a disqualification.

The Winners Dog and Winners Bitch are the two that are awarded the points for their breed. They then go on to compete with any champions of record (often called "specials") of their breed that are entered in the show. The champions may be dogs or bitches; in this class, all are shown together. The judge reviews the Winners Dog and Winners Bitch along with all of the champions to select the Best of Breed winner. The Best of Winners is selected between the Winners Dog and Winners Bitch; if one of these two is selected Best of Breed as well,

Junior showmanship provides children with an excellent way to spend time with their best friends.

he or she is automatically determined Best of Winners. Lastly, the judge selects Best of Opposite Sex to the Best of Breed winner. The Best of Breed winner then goes on to the group competition.

At a group or all-breed show, the Best of Breed winners from each breed are divided into their respective groups to compete against one another for Group One through Group Four. Group One (first place) is awarded to the dog that best lives up to the ideal for his breed as described in the

JUNIOR SHOWMANSHIP

For budding dog handlers, ages 10 to 18 years, Junior Showmanship competitions are an excellent training ground for the next generation of dog professionals. Owning and caring for a dog are wonderful methods of teaching children responsibility, and Junior Showmanship builds upon that foundation. Juniors learn by grooming, handling and training their dogs, and the quality of a junior's presentation of the dog (and himself) is evaluated by a licensed judge. The junior can enter with any registered AKC dog to compete, including an Indefinite Listing Privilege, provided that the dog lives with him or a member of his family.

Junior Showmanship competitions are divided into two classes: Novice (for beginners) and Open (for juniors who have three first place wins in the Novice Class). The junior must run with the dog with the rest of the handlers and dogs, stack the dog for examination and individually gait the dog in a specific pattern. Juniors should practice with a handling class or an experienced handler before entering the Novice Class so that they recognize all the jargon that the judge may use.

A National Junior Organization was founded in 1997 to help promote the sport of dog showing among young people. The AKC also offers a Junior Scholarship for juniors who excel in the program.

standard. A group judge, therefore, must have a thorough working knowledge of many breed standards. After placements have been made in each group, the seven Group One winners (from the Sporting Group, Toy Group, Hound Group, etc.) compete against each other for the top honor, Best in Show.

There are different ways to find out about dog shows in your area. The American Kennel Club's monthly magazine, the *AKC Gazette* is accompanied by, the *Events Calendar*; this magazine is available through subscription. You can also look on the AKC's and your parent club's websites for information and check the event listings in your local newspaper.

Your Ibizan Hound must be six months of age or older and registered with the AKC in order to be entered in AKC-sanctioned shows in which there are classes for the Ibizan Hound. Your Ibizan Hound also must not possess any disqualifying faults and must be sexually intact. The reason for the latter is simple: dog shows are the proving grounds to determine which dogs and bitches are worthy of being bred. If they cannot be bred, that defeats the purpose! On that note, only dogs that have achieved championships, thus proving their excellent quality, should be bred. If you have spayed or neutered your dog, however, there are many AKC events other

than conformation, such as obedience trials, agility trials and the Canine Good Citizen® Program, in which you and your Ibizan Hound can participate.

OBEDIENCE TRIALS

Mrs. Helen Whitehouse Walker, a Standard Poodle fancier, can be credited with introducing obedience trials to the United States. In the 1930s she designed a series of exercises based on those of the Associated Sheep, Police, Army Dog Society of Great Britain. These exercises were intended to evaluate the working relationship between dog and owner. Since those early days of the sport in the US, obedience trials have grown more and more popular, and now more than 2,000 trials each year attract over 100,000 dogs and their owners. Any dog registered with the AKC, regardless of neutering or other disqualifications that would preclude entry in conformation competition, can participate in obedience trials.

There are three levels of difficulty in obedience competition. The first (and easiest) level is the Novice, in which dogs can earn the Companion Dog (CD) title. The intermediate level is the Open level, in which the Companion Dog Excellent (CDX) title is awarded. The advanced level is the Utility level, in which dogs compete for the Utility Dog (UD) title. Classes at each level are

Each of these handsome Ibizans is waiting to be examined by the judge. What an impressive line-up!

further divided into "A" and "B," with "A" for beginners and "B" for those with more experience. In order to win a title at a given level, a dog must earn three "legs." A "leg" is accomplished when a dog scores 170 or higher (200 is a perfect score). The scoring system gets a little trickier when you understand that a dog must score more than 50% of the points available for each exercise in order to actually earn the points. Available points for each exercise range between 20 and 40.

A dog must complete different exercises at each level of obedience. The Novice exercises are the easiest, with the Open and finally the Utility levels progressing in difficulty. Examples of Novice exercises are on- and off-lead heeling, a figure-8 pattern, performing a recall (or come), long sit and long down and standing for examination. In the Open level, the Novice-level exercises are required again, but this time without a leash and for longer durations. In addition, the dog must clear a broad jump, retrieve over a jump and drop on recall. In the Utility level, the exercises are quite

BECOMING A CHAMPION

An official AKC championship of record requires that a dog accumulate 15 points under 3 different judges, including 2 "majors" under different judges. Points are awarded based on the number of dogs entered into competition, varying from breed to breed and place to place. A win of three, four or five points is considered a "major." The AKC annually assigns a schedule of points to adjust for variations that accompany a breed's popularity and the population of a given area.

difficult, including executing basic commands based on hand signals, following a complex heeling pattern, locating articles based on scent discrimination and completing jumps at the handler's direction.

Once he's earned the UD title, a dog can go on to win the prestigious title of Utility Dog Excellent (UDX) by winning "legs" in ten shows. Additionally, Utility Dogs who win "legs" in Open B and Utility B earn points toward the lofty title of Obedience Trial Champion (OTCh.). Established in 1977 by the AKC, this title requires a dog to earn 100 points as well as 3 first places in a combination of Open B and Utility B classes under 3 different judges. The "brass ring" of obedience competition is the AKC's National Obedience Invitational. This is an exclusive competition for only the cream of the obedience crop. In order to qualify for the invitational, a dog must be ranked in either the top 25 all-breeds in obedience or in the top 3 for his breed in obedience. The title at stake here is that of National Obedience Champion (NOC).

AGILITY TRIALS

Agility trials became sanctioned by the American Kennel Club in August 1994, when the first licensed agility trials were held. Since that time, agility certainly has grown in popularity by leaps

and bounds, literally! The AKC allows all registered breeds (including Miscellaneous Class breeds) to participate, providing the dog is 12 months of age or

DRESS THE PART

It's a dog show, so don't forget your costume. Even though the show is about the dog, you also must play your role well. You have been cast as the "dog handler" and you must smartly dress the part. Solid colors make a nice complement to the dog's coat, but choose colors that contrast. You don't want to be wearing a solid color that blends mostly or entirely with the major or only color of your dog. Whether the show is indoors or out, you still must dress properly. You want the judge to perceive you as being professional, so polish, polish, polish! And don't forget to wear sensible shoes; remember, you have to gait around the ring with your dog.

Show dogs are gaited in the ring so that the judge can evaluate the dog's movement. Proper structure leads to proper movement, and this is important in a quick, agile sighthound breed.

older. Agility is designed so that the handler demonstrates how well the dog can work at his side. The handler directs his dog through, over, under and around an obstacle course that includes jumps, tires, the dog walk, weave poles, pipe tunnels, collapsed tunnels and more. While working his way through the course, the dog must keep one eye and ear on the handler and the rest of his body on the course. The handler runs along with the dog, giving verbal and hand signals to guide the dog through the course.

The first organization to promote agility trials in the US was the United States Dog Agility Association, Inc. (USDAA). Established in 1986, the USDAA sparked the formation of many member clubs around the country. To participate in USDAA trials, dogs must be at least 18 months of age.

The USDAA and AKC both offer titles to winning dogs, although the exercises and requirements of the two organizations differ. Agility Dog (AD), Advanced Agility Dog (AAD) and Master Agility Dog (MAD) are the titles

CANINE GOOD CITIZEN® PROGRAM

Have you ever considered getting your dog "certified"? The AKC's Canine Good Citizen® Program affords your dog just that opportunity. Your dog shows that he is a well-behaved canine citizen, using the basic training and good manners you have taught him, by taking a series of ten tests that illustrate that he can behave properly at home, in a public place and around other dogs. The tests are administered by participating dog clubs, colleges, 4-H clubs, Scouts and other community groups and are open to all pure-bred and mixed-breed dogs. Upon passing the ten tests, the suffix CGC is then applied to your dog's name.

The ten tests are: 1. Accepting a friendly stranger; 2. Sitting politely for petting; 3. Appearance and grooming; 4. Walking on a lead; 5. Walking through a group of people; 6. Sit, down and stay on command; 7. Coming when called; 8. Meeting another dog; 9. Calm reaction to distractions; 10. Separation from owner.

offered by the USDAA, while the AKC offers Novice Agility (NA), Open Agility (OA), Agility Excellent (AX) and Master Agility Excellent (MX). Beyond these four AKC titles, dogs can win additional titles in "jumper" classes: Jumper with Weave Novice (NAJ), Open (OAJ) and Excellent (MXJ). The ultimate title in AKC agility is MACH, Master Agility Champion. Dogs can continue to add number designations to the MACH title, indicating how many times the dog has met the title's requirements (MACH1, MACH2 and so on).

Agility trials are a great way to keep your dog active, and they will keep you running, too! You should join a local agility club to learn more about the sport. These clubs offer sessions in which you can introduce your dog to the various obstacles as well as training classes to prepare him for competition. In no time, your dog will be climbing A-frames, crossing the dog walk and flying over hurdles, all with you right beside him.

TRACKING

Tracking tests are exciting ways to test your Ibizan Hound's instinctive scenting ability on a competitive level. All dogs have a nose, and all breeds are welcome in tracking tests. The first AKC-

When it comes to tracking, the Ibizan is a no-nonsense hound.

licensed tracking test took place in 1937 as part of the Utility level at an obedience trial, and thus competitive tracking was officially begun. The first title, Tracking Dog (TD), was offered in 1947, ten years after the first official tracking test. It was not until 1980 that the AKC added the title Tracking Dog Excellent (TDX), which was followed by the title Variable Surface Tracking (VST) in 1995. Champion Tracker (CT) is awarded to a dog who has earned all three of those titles.

The TD level is the first and most basic level in tracking, progressing in difficulty to the TDX and then the VST. A dog must follow a track laid by a human 30 to 120 minutes prior in order to earn the TD title. The track is about 500 yards long and contains up to 5 directional changes. At the next level, the TDX, the dog must follow a 3- to 5-hour-old track over a course that is up to 1,000 yards long and has up to 7 directional changes. In the most difficult level, the VST, the track is up to 5 hours old and located in an urban setting.

LURE COURSING
Owners of sighthound breeds have the opportunity to participate in lure coursing. Lure-coursing events are exciting and fast-paced,

The appeal of lure coursing is seeing these beautiful hounds, with their remarkable speed and graceful movement, performing at what they instinctively do best.

requiring dogs to follow an artificial lure around a course on an open field. Scores are based on the dog's speed, enthusiasm, agility, endurance and ability to follow the lure. At the non-competitive level, lure coursing is designed to gauge a sighthound's instinctive coursing ability. Competitive lure coursing is more demanding, requiring training and conditioning for a dog to develop his coursing instincts and skills to the fullest, thus preserving the intended function of all sighthound breeds. Breeds eligible for AKC lure coursing are the Ibizan Hound, Whippet, Basenji, Greyhound, Italian Greyhound, Afghan Hound, Borzoi, Pharaoh Hound, Irish Wolfhound, Scottish Deerhound, Saluki and Rhodesian Ridgeback.

Lure coursing on a competitive level is certainly wonderful physical and mental exercise for a dog. A dog must be at least one year of age to enter an AKC coursing event, and he must not have any disqualifications according to his breed standard. Check the AKC's rules and regulations for details. To get started, you can consult the AKC's website to help you find a coursing club in your area. A club can introduce you to the sport and help you learn how to train your dog correctly.

Titles awarded in lure coursing are Junior Courser (JC),

> **AKC GROUPS**
> For showing purposes, the American Kennel Club divides its recognized breeds into seven groups: Sporting Dogs, Hounds, Working Dogs, Terriers, Toys, Non-Sporting Dogs and Herding Dogs.

Senior Courser (SC) and Master Courser (MC); these are suffix titles, affixed to the end of the dog's name. The Field Champion (FC) title is a prefix title, affixed to the beginning of the dog's name. A Dual Champion is a hound that has earned both a Field Champion title as well as a show championship. A Triple Champion (TC) title is awarded to a dog that is a Champion, Field Champion and Obedience Trial Champion. The suffix Lure Courser Excellent (LCX) is given to a dog who has earned the FC title plus 45 additional championship points, and number designations are added to the title upon each additional 45 championship points earned (LCX II, III, IV and so on).

Sighthounds also can participate in events sponsored by the American Sighthound Field Association (ASFA), an organization devoted to the pursuit of lure coursing. The ASFA was founded in 1972 as a means of keeping open field coursing dogs fit in the off-season. It has grown into the largest lure-coursing association in the world. Dogs must be of an accepted sighthound breed in order to be eligible for participation. Each dog must pass a certification run in which he shows that he can run with another dog without interfering. The course is laid out using pulleys and a motor to drive the string around the pulleys. Normally white plastic bags are used as lures, although real fur strips may also be attached. Dogs run in trios, each handled by their own slipper. The dogs are scored on their endurance, follow, speed, agility and enthusiasm. Dogs earn their Field Champion titles by earning 2 first places, or 1 first- and 2 second-place finishes, as well as accumulating 100 points. They can then go on to earn the LCM title, Lure Courser of Merit, by winning 4 first places and accumulating 300 additional points.

Coursing is an all-day event, held in all weather conditions. It is great fun for the whole family, but on a rainy, cold day, it's best to leave the kids at home!

RACING

The Large Gazehound Racing Association (LGRA) and the National Oval Track Racing Association (NOTRA) are organizations that sponsor and regulate dog races. Races are usually either 200-yard sprints

(LGRA) or semi- or complete ovals (NOTRA). Both of these organizations allow most sighthound breeds except Whippets to participate. (Whippets have their own racing organizations exclusively for the breed.) In both LGRA and NOTRA races, the dogs generally run out of starting boxes, meaning that racing dogs must be trained to the box. Local racing clubs offer training programs that can assist novice owners and dogs.

Dogs compete in a draw of four each and are ranked according to their previous racing record. The lure in LGRA events consists of both real fur and a predator call. In NOTRA events, the lure is white plastic and often a fur strip. There are three programs and the dogs are rotated through the draw according to their finish in each preceding program. Dogs earn the Gazehound Racing Champion (GRC) or the Oval Racing Champion (ORC) title when they accumulate 15 race points. Dogs can go on to earn the Superior titles by accumulating 30 additional points.

Both LGRA and NOTRA races are owner-participation sports in which each owner plays some role: catcher, walker, line judge or foul judge. If you plan to race your dog, plan to work all day during a race day. There is little time for anything else, but the reward of seeing four dogs pour over the finish line shoulder to shoulder is more than enough.

The bottom line is this: there is so much to do with your dog that it can be hard to decide which event to try. Just as we have to choose what to do with our weekends, so do the dogs. Whatever you choose to do with your dog, it will take training, dedication and a willingness to work with your dog to achieve a common goal, a partnership between you and your dog. There is nothing more pleasing than to watch a handler and dog performing at a high level, whether it is the show ring or the field. There is something for everyone and every dog in the world of dog "showing." Dog showing should really be called "competing with your dog." You are not restricted to the traditional "dog show" and may find that your "show dog" excels in other areas as well or instead.

No matter what activity you choose for your Ibizan, with proper devotion to his training he will succeed and will enjoy spending time doing things with you.

You chose your dog because something clicked the minute you set eyes on him. Or perhaps it seemed that the dog selected you and that's what clinched the deal. Either way, you are now investing time and money in this dog, a true pal and an outstanding member of the family. Everything about him is perfect—well, almost perfect. Remember, he is a dog! For that matter, how does he think *you're* doing?

UNDERSTANDING THE CANINE MINDSET

For starters, you and your dog are on different wavelengths. Your dog is similar to a toddler in that

both live in the present tense only. A dog's view of life is based primarily on cause and effect, which is similar to the old saying, "Nothing teaches a youngster to hang on like falling off the swing." If your dog stumbles down a flight of three steps, the next time he will try the Superman approach and fling himself off the top one!

Your dog makes connections based on the fact that he lives in the present, so when he is doing something and you interrupt to dispense praise or a correction, a connection, positive or negative, is made. To the dog, that's like one plus one equals two! In the same sense, it's also easy to see that when your timing is off, you will cause an incorrect connection. The one-plus-one way of thinking is why you must never scold a dog for behavior that took place an hour, 15 minutes or even 5 seconds ago. But it is also why, when your timing is perfect, you can teach him to do all kinds of wonderful things—as soon as he has made that essential connection. What helps the process is his desire to please you and to have your approval.

No one enjoys living with a food thief. You must train your Ibizan to respect the boundaries you set or else you'll be sharing your meal whether you like it or not.

There are behaviors we admire in dogs, such as friendliness and obedience, as well as those behaviors that cause problems to a varying degree. The dog owner who encounters minor behavioral problems is wise to solve them promptly or get professional help. Bad behaviors are not corrected by repeatedly shouting "No" or getting angry with the dog. Only the giving of praise and approval for good behavior lets your dog understand right from wrong. The longer a bad behavior is allowed to continue, the harder it is to overcome. A responsible breeder is often able to help. Each dog is unique, so try not to compare your dog's behavior with your neighbor's dog or the one you had as a child.

Have your veterinarian check the dog to see whether a behavior problem could have a physical cause. An earache or toothache, for example, could be the reason for a dog to snap at you if you were to touch his head when putting on his leash. A sharp correction from you would only increase the behavior. When a physical basis is eliminated, and if the problem is not something you understand or can cope with, ask for the name of a behavioral specialist, preferably one who is familiar with the Ibizan Hound. Be sure to keep the breeder informed of your progress.

Many things, such as environment and inherited traits, form the basic behavior of a dog, just as in humans. You also must factor into his temperament the purpose for which your dog was originally bred. The major obstacle lies in the dog's inability to explain his behavior to us in a way that we understand. The one thing you should not do is to give up and abandon your dog. Somewhere a

The nose knows. A dog will use his nose to investigate new acquaintances, a proper social behavior among canines.

LOOK AT ME WHEN I SPEAK TO YOU

Your dog considers direct eye contact as a sign of dominance. A shy dog will avoid looking at you; a dominant dog will try to stare you down. What you want is for your dog to pay attention when you speak, and that doesn't necessarily involve direct eye contact. In dealing with a problem dog, avert your gaze momentarily, return to face the dog and give an immediate down command. Show him that you're the boss.

It is normal for canines to be more physical in play. Interaction between children and your Ibizan should be supervised, and they must be taught how to play properly with one another.

pleasant to see bared teeth or to hear your dog growl or snarl, but these are signs of behavior that, if left uncorrected, can become extremely dangerous. A word of warning here: never challenge an aggressive dog. He is unpredictable and therefore unreliable to approach.

Nothing gets a "hello" from strangers on the street quicker than walking a puppy, but people should ask permission before petting your dog so you can tell him to sit in order to receive the admiring pats. If a hand comes down over the dog's head and he shrinks back, ask the person to bring their hand up, underneath the pup's chin. Now you're correcting strangers, too! But if you don't, it could make your dog afraid of strangers, which in turn can lead to fear-biting. Socialization prevents much aggression before it rears its ugly head.

The body language of an aggressive dog about to attack is clear. The dog will have a hard, steady stare. He will try to look as big as possible by standing stiff-legged, pushing out his chest, keeping his ears up and holding his tail up and steady. The hackles on his back will rise so that a ridge of hairs stands up. This posture may include the curled lip, snarl and/or growl, or he may be silent. He looks, and definitely is, very dangerous.

misunderstanding has occurred but, with help and patient understanding on your part, you should be able to work out the majority of bothersome behaviors.

AGGRESSION

"Aggression" is a word that is often misunderstood and is sometimes even used to describe what is actually normal canine behavior. For example, it's normal for puppies to growl when playing tug-of-war. It's puppy talk. There are different forms of dog aggression, but all are degrees of dominance, indicating that the dog, not his master, is (or thinks he is) in control. When the dog feels that he (or his control of the situation) is threatened, he will respond. The extent of the aggressive behavior varies with individual dogs. It is not at all

This dominant posture is seen in dogs that are territorially aggressive. Deliverymen are constant victims of serious bites from such dogs. Territorial aggression is the reason you should never, ever try to train a puppy to be a watchdog. It can escalate into this type of behavior over which you will have no control. All forms of aggression must be taken seriously and dealt with immediately. If signs of aggressive behavior continue, or grow worse, or if you are at all unsure about how to deal with your dog's behavior, get the help of a professional.

Uncontrolled aggression, sometimes called "irritable aggression," is not something for the pet owner to try to solve. If you cannot solve your dog's dangerous behavior with professional help, and you (quite rightly) do not wish to keep a canine time-bomb in your home, you will have some important decisions to make. Aggressive dogs often cannot be rehomed successfully, as they are dangerous and unreliable in their behavior. An aggressive dog should be dealt with only by someone who knows exactly the situation that he is getting into and has the experience, dedication and ideal living environment to attempt rehabilitating the dog, which often is not possible. In these cases, the dog ends up having to be humanely put down.

Making a decision about euthanasia is not an easy undertaking for anyone, for any reason, but you cannot pass on to another home a dog that you know could cause harm.

A milder form of aggression is the dog's guarding anything that he perceives to be his—his food dish, his toys, his bed and/or his crate. This can be prevented if you take firm control from the start. The young puppy can and should be taught that his leader will share, but that certain rules apply. Guarding is mild aggression only

MINE! MINE! MINE!
Let's face it. The only possessions a dog has are the ones that his humans give him. That said, a dog may develop the tendency to jealously guard the things that are "his." At the first sign of possessive behavior (steady stare, head lowered, growling), either call him cheerfully, "Come," and move away, or ignore him altogether. Don't try to take away whatever is in his possession.

PHOTOGRAPHY BY CAROL BEUCHAT

Try a simple distraction first, such as tossing a toy or picking up his leash for a walk. If that doesn't work, the best way to handle the situation is with basic obedience. Show the dog a treat, followed by calm, almost slow-motion commands: "Come. Sit. Drop it. Good dog," and then hand over the cheese! That's one example of positive- reinforcement training.

Children can be bitten when they try to retrieve a stolen shoe or toy, so they need to know how to handle the dog or to let an adult do it. They may also be bitten as they run away from a dog, in either fear or play. The dog sees the child's running as reason for pursuit, and even a friendly young puppy will nip at the heels of a runaway. Teach the kids not to run away from a strange dog and when to stop overly exciting play with their own puppy.

in the beginning stages, and it will worsen and become dangerous if you let it.

Don't try to snatch anything away from your puppy. Bargain for the item in question so that you can positively reinforce him when he gives it up. Punishment only results in worsening any aggressive behavior.

Many dogs extend their guarding impulse toward items they've stolen. The dog figures, "If I have it, it's mine!" (Some ill-behaved kids have similar tendencies.) An angry confrontation will only increase the dog's aggression. (Have you ever watched a child have a tantrum?)

Fear-biting is yet another aggressive behavior. A fear-biter gives many warning signals. The dog leans away from the approaching person (sometimes hiding behind his owner) with his ears and tail down, but not in submission. He may even shiver. His hackles are raised, his lips curled. When the person steps into the dog's "flight zone" (a circle of 1 to 3 feet surrounding the dog), he attacks. Because of the fear factor, he performs a rapid attack-and-retreat. Because it is directed at a person, vets are often the victims of this form of aggression. It is frightening, but discovering and eliminating the cause of the fright will help overcome the dog's need to bite. Early socialization again plays a strong role in the prevention of this behavior. Again, if you can't cope with it, get the help of an expert.

SEPARATION ANXIETY

Any behaviorist will tell you that separation anxiety is the most common problem about which pet owners complain. It is also one of the easiest to prevent. Unfortunately, a behaviorist usually is not consulted until the dog is a stressed-out, neurotic mess. At that stage, it is indeed a problem that requires the help of a professional.

Training the puppy to the fact that people in the house come and go is essential in order to avoid this anxiety. Leaving the puppy in his crate or a confined area while family members go in and out, and stay out for longer and longer periods of time, is the basic way to desensitize the pup to the family's frequent departures. If you are at home most of every day, make it a point to go out for at least an hour or two whenever possible.

How you leave is vital to the dog's reaction. Your dog is no fool. He knows the difference

between sweats and business suits, jeans and dresses. He sees you pat your pocket to check for your wallet, open your briefcase, check that you have your cell phone or pick up the car keys. He knows from the hurry of the kids in the morning that they're off to school until afternoon. Lipstick? Aftershave lotion? Lunch boxes? Every move you make registers in

I CAN'T SMILE WITHOUT YOU

How can you tell whether your dog is suffering from separation anxiety? Not every dog who enjoys a close bond with his owner will suffer from separation anxiety. In actuality, only a small percentage of dogs is affected. Separation anxiety manifests itself in dogs older than one year of age and may not occur until the dog is a senior. A number of destructive behaviors are associated with the problem, including scratch marks in front of doorways, bite marks on furniture, drool stains on furniture and flooring and tattered draperies, carpets or cushions. The most reliable sign of separation anxiety is howling and crying when the owner leaves and then barking like mad for extended periods. Affected dogs may also defecate or urinate throughout the home, attempt to escape when the door opens, vocalize excessively and show signs of depression (including loss of appetite, listlessness and lack of activity).

Left with a safe chew toy and a comfortable place to nap, your Ibizan won't have a chance to miss you.

his sensory perception and memory. Your puppy knows more about your departures than you do. You can't get away with a thing!

Before you got dressed, you checked the dog's water bowl and his supply of toys (including a long-lasting chew toy), and turned the radio on low. You will leave him in what he considers his "safe" area, not with total freedom of the house. If you've invested in child safety gates, you can be

reasonably sure that he'll remain in the designated area. Don't give him access to a window where he can watch you leave the house. If you're leaving for an hour or two, just put him into his crate with a safe toy.

Now comes the test! You are ready to walk out the door. Do not give your Ibizan Hound a big hug and a fond farewell. Do not drag out a long goodbye. Those are the very things that jump-start separation anxiety. Toss a biscuit into the dog's area, call out "So long, pooch" and close the door. You're gone. The chances are that the dog may bark a couple of times, or maybe whine once or twice, and then settle down to enjoy his biscuit and take a lovely nap, especially if you took him for a nice long walk after breakfast. As he grows up, the barks and whines will stop because it's an old routine, so why should he make the effort?

When you first brought home the puppy, the come-and-go routine was intermittent and constant. He was put into his crate with a tiny treat. You left (silently) and returned in 3 minutes, then 5, then 10, then 15, then half an hour, until finally you could leave without a problem and be gone for 2 or 3 hours. If, at any time in the future, there's a "separation" problem, refresh his memory by going back to that basic training.

Now comes the next most important part—your return. Do not make a big production of coming home. "Hi, poochie" is as grand a greeting as he needs. When you've taken off your hat and coat, tossed your briefcase on the hall table and glanced at the mail, and the dog has settled down from the excitement of seeing you "in person" from his confined area, then go and give him a warm, friendly greeting. A potty trip is needed and a walk would be appreciated, since he's been such a good dog.

DIGGING

Digging is another natural and normal doggie behavior. Wild canines dig to bury whatever food they can save for later to

> ## DIGGING OUT
> Some dogs love to dig. Others wouldn't think of it. Digging is considered "self-rewarding behavior" because it's fun! Of all the digging solutions offered by the experts, most are only marginally successful and none is guaranteed to work. The best cure is prevention, which means removing the dog from the offending site when he digs as well as distracting him when you catch him digging so that he turns his attentions elsewhere. That means that you have to supervise your dog's yard time. An unsupervised digger can create havoc with your landscaping or, worse, run away!

eat. (And you thought *we* invented the doggie bag!) Burying bones or toys is a primary cause to dig. Dogs also dig to get at interesting little underground creatures like moles and mice. In the summer, they dig to get down to cool earth. In winter, they dig to get beneath the cold surface to warmer earth.

The solution to the last two is easy. In the summer, provide a bed that's up off the ground and placed in a shaded area. In winter, the dog should either be indoors to sleep or given an adequate insulated doghouse outdoors. To understand how natural and normal this is you have only to consider the Nordic breeds of sled dog who, at the end of the run, routinely dig a bed for themselves in the snow. It's the nesting instinct. How often have you seen your dog go round and round in circles, pawing at his blanket or bedding before flopping down to sleep?

Domesticated dogs also dig to escape, and that's a lot more dangerous than it is destructive. A dog that digs under the fence is the one that is hit by a car or becomes lost. A good fence to protect a digger should be set 10 to 12 inches below ground level, and every fence needs to be routinely checked for even the smallest openings that can become possible escape routes.

The tendency to dig varies from dog to dog. When it occurs, it is a behavior you need to discourage or at least control.

Catching your dog in the act of digging is the easiest way to stop it, because your dog will make the "one-plus-one" connection, but digging is too often a solitary occupation, something the lonely dog does out of boredom. Catch your young puppy in the act and put a stop to it before you have a yard full of craters. It is more difficult to stop if your dog sees you gardening. If you can dig, why can't he? Because you say so, that's why! Some dogs are excavation experts, and some dogs never dig. However, when it comes to any of these instinctive canine behaviors, never say "never."

FOOD-RELATED PROBLEMS

We're not talking about eating, diets or nutrition here, we're talking about bad habits. Face it. All dogs are beggars. Food is the motivation for everything we want our dogs to do and, when you combine that with their innate ability to "con" us in order to get their way, it's a wonder there aren't far more obese dogs in the world.

Who can resist the bleeding-heart look that says "I'm starving," the paw that gently pats your knee and gives you a knowing look, the whining "please" or even the total body language of a perfect sit beneath the cookie jar. No one who professes to love his dog can turn down the pleas of his clever canine's performances every time. One thing is for sure, though: definitely do not allow begging at the table. Family meals do not include your dog.

Control your dog's begging habit by making your dog work for his rewards. Ignore his begging when you can. Utilize the obedience commands you've taught your dog. Use "Off" for the pawing. A sit or even a long down will interrupt the whining. His reward in these situations is definitely not a treat! Casual verbal praise is enough. Be sure all members of the family follow the same rules. There is a different type of begging that does demand your immediate response and that is the appeal to be let (or taken) outside! Usually that is a quick paw or small whine to get your attention, followed by a race to the door. This type of begging needs your quick attention and approval. Of course, a really smart dog will soon figure out how to cut you off at the pass and direct you to that cookie jar on your way to the door. Some dogs are always one step ahead of us.

Stealing food is a problem only if you are not paying attention. A dog can't steal food that is not within his reach. Leaving your dog in the kitchen with the roast beef on the table is asking for trouble. Nothing idiopathic about this problem, though perhaps a little idiotic! Putting cheese and crackers on the coffee table also requires a watchful eye to stop the thief in his tracks. The word to use (one word, remember, even if it's two words pronounced as one) is "Leave it!" Instead of preceding it with yet another "No," try using a guttural sound like "Aagh!" That sounds more like a warning growl to the dog and therefore has instant meaning.

Canine thieves are in their element when little kids are carrying cookies in their hands! Your dog will think he's been

exceptionally clever if he causes a child to drop a cookie. Bonanza! The easiest solution is to keep dog and children separated at snack time. You must also be sure that the children understand that they must not tease the dog with food—his or theirs. Your dog does not mean to bite the kids, but when he snatches at a tidbit so near the level of his mouth, it can result in an unintended nip.

LEAPING IBIZANS

The Ibizan Hound is a great jumper, capable of jumping great distances in both height and length. From a standstill, he can leap between 6 and 8 feet straight up in the air! In straight racing an Ibizan has been known to run at 40 miles per hour.

Because of the Ibizan Hound's prowess as a jumper, it is essential that fencing is at least 6 feet high. And perimeter fencing is very important around your property and exercise area, for if an Ibizan Hound escapes it can be a good distance away before you have had time to blink! Keep in mind that this breed has a justified reputation as an escapologist.

PHOTOGRAPHY BY CAROL BEUCHAT.

INDEX

Activities 104
Adenovirus 115
Adult
—adoption 86
—feeding 65
—health 111
—training 85-86
Aggression 54, 87, 116, 148-151
Agility 105, 139-141
Aging 111
AKC Gazette 137
Allergies 24
Alpha 93
Amar kennels 17
American Kennel Club 15-16,
 129, 131, 133, 139, 143
—breed standard 21, 28, 35
—championship 138
American Sighthound Field
 Association 17
Ancylostoma caninum **124, 125**
Anemia 67
Anesthetics 23
Anita of Chardia 13
Annual vet exams 111
Antifreeze 50
Anubis 8, 9
Appearance 18
Appetite loss 109
Ascarid **124, 125**
Ascaris lumbricoides **124**
Atakah kennels 17
Atakah's Flying Cub 17
Attention 94, 96, 102
Australia 17
Balearic Greyhound 12
Ballard, Wendy 82
Bathing 72
Bedding 43, 53, 90
Begging 154, 155
Behavior 146-155
—specialist 147, 151
Berry, Diana 14
Bite 21
Biting 150
Bloat 70
Blushing 23
Boarding 81, 82
Body language 87, 91, 98, 148-
 149, 154
Body temperature 111
Bones 43
Bordetella 115
Bordetella bronchiseptica 116

Boredom 22, 154
Borrelia burgdorferi 115
Borreliosis 116
Bowls 41
Breed purpose 10-11
Breed standard 28
Breeder
—selection 107
Breeding 35
Bushland Issa of Curtis Lane
 16
Bylandt, Count Henry 12
Canadian Kennel Club 129
Cancer 116
Canine cough 115
Canine Good Citizen® Program
 137, 140
Center for the Human-Animal
 Bond 25
Certera 14
Charnegue 12
Cheyletiella mites 122
Chew toys 43-44, 59, 89-90
Chewing 43, 58
Chiggers 123
Children 20, 25, 52, 54, 58, 61,
 87, 150, 155
Classes 134, 135
Coat 22
Cognitive dysfunction 112
Collar 45, 47, 80, 94
Color 22
Come 61, 101
Command 96
—potty 93
—practicing 97, 100
Commitment of ownership
 40, 56
Consistency 55, 60, 92, 96
Core vaccines 116
Coronavirus 115-116
Correction 94, 146
Crate 41, 52-53, 61, 89, 151
—pads 43
Crufts 13, 14
Crying 53, 61, 90
Ctenocephalides canis **118**
Dangers in the home 46, 50
Deafness 23, 24
DEET 123
Demodex folliculoram **122**
Demodex mites 123
Dental care 76-77, 109, 111
Destructive behavior 151

Diet 24
—adult 65
—puppy 63
—senior 66
Digging 153, 154
Dipylidium canium 125
Dirofilaria immitis **125**
Discipline 57, 61, 93
Distemper 115-116
Dog flea 118
DogGone™ newsletter 82
Dominance 97, 147-149
Down 60, 91, 97-98
Down/stay 100
Ears 21, 75, 76
Edwards, Richard 16
Egypt 17
English Ibizan Hound Club 13
Eridu Maestro of Loki 16
Escaping 153
Estrus 116
Events Calendar 137
Excessive thirst 68
Exercise 70-71
—pen 89
Expenses of ownership 37
External parasites 118-123
Eyes 21
—disorders 26
—contact 147
Family
—meeting the puppy 52
Fear 54, 155
—biting 148, 150
—period 54
Feeding 63-68
—adult 65-66
—puppy 63-65
—schedule 64
Fence 16, 50, 153, 155
Field trials 17
First night in new home 52
Flea **118, 119**, 120
Food 89
—bowls 41
—loss of interest in 109
—poisonous to dogs 67
—rewards 86, 96, 103
—types 67
Food stealing 155
Forequarters 21
Free lee Preu, Mr. and Mrs. 15
Gait 22
Gastric torsion 70

Genetic testing 107
Giardia 115
Grinder for nails 74
Gryphon's Stellar Eminence
 135
Grooming 71-79
Guarding 149
Gum disease 109
Hannibal (Stop) 10
Hannibal 14
Health 23
—adult 111
—benefits of dog ownership
 19
—insurance for pets 113
—journal 52
—puppy 39, 51, 107
—senior dog 111
Heart disease 112
Heartworm 109, **125**, 126, **127**
Heat cycle 116
Heel 102-103
Height 12, 22
Hemato's J-Mark Star Maiden
 15
Hepatitis 115-116
Herding trials 105
Hereditary problems 23
Heterodoxus spiniger **122**
Hindquarters 21
Hip dysplasia 26-27
Homemade toys 45
Hookworm **124, 125**
House-training 42, 53, 87-88,
 93, 95
—puppy needs 88
—schedule 90, 92
Hunderassen 12
Hunting 11, 105
Ibia of Loki 16
Ibiza 9
Ibizan Hound Club of the
 United States 15, 16, 28, 133
Ibizan Hound Club of America
 15
Ibizan Hound Fanciers and
 Exhibitors of the United
 States 15
Identification 79-81
Infectious diseases 114
Injections 25
Insecticides, sensitivity to 25
Insurance 113
Internal parasites 124-127

Irritable aggression 149
Ishtar Alpha Ra-de Koo Kay 16
Ishtar Charisma 16
Ishtar Sonnet of Loki 16
Ishtar Threehand Aquilla of
 O'Bre-on's 16
Ixodes dammini **120**, **121**
Judge 128-129
Jumping up 18, 59, 91, 155
Junior showmanship 136
Kennel Club, The 13, 28, 129
Kennel Review Top Producer
 award 16
Kidney problems 112
King Tut's Nefertiti **14**
Leash 46, 48, 94-95
—pulling on 103
Leighton, Robert 12, 13
Leptospirosis 115-116
Lifespan 111
Loneliness 151
Lost dog 80
Louse **122**
Lure coursing 17, 22, 105, 142-
 144
Luxor's Playmate of the Year
 16, **134**
Lyme disease 116
Malchus V 15
Mammary cancer 116
Mating 10
Maya 16
Microchip 80, 81
Mindset of dogs 146
Miscellaneous Class 15
Mites **121**, **122**, 123
Monorchidism 25
Mosquitoes 123
Mounting 116
Multi-dog household 70
Murphy, Mariette 17
Muzzle 21
Nail clipping 73-74
Name 96, 102
Neutering 51, 109, 116-117
New Book of the Dog, The 12
Nipping 58, 61
Non-core vaccines 116
Nose 21
Obedience 99, 104, 137-139
Off 60, 91
Okay 99, 103
Olives de Cotonera, Dona
 Maria Dolores 12, 15, 16
Origins 8
Orthopedic Foundation for
 Animals 26
Other dogs 70, 116

Other pets 20, 87
Outdoor safety 50, 153
Ovariohysterectomy 116-117
Ownership 40, 56
—expenses of 37
—health benefits of 19
Pack animals 55
Paper-training 88, 91
Parainfluenza 116
Parasite
—control 25, 109
—external 118-123
—internal 124-127
Parvovirus 115-116
Patella luxation 26
Patience 87, 96
PennHIP 26
Personality 18
Petra of Chardia 13
Phoenicians 9
Physical characteristics 21, **22**
Podenco Andaluz 9, **10**
Podenco Canario 9
Podenco Ibicenco 9
Podengo 13
Podengo Portuguêse 9, **13**
Poisons 50, 67
Portuguese Warren Hounds **12**
Positive reinforcement 52, 93,
 96, 146, 150
Possessive behavior 149
Practicing 100
—commands 97
Praise 86, 93, 96, 104, 146-147
Preventive care 107, 111-112
Problem behavior 147
Prostate problems 116
Punishment 18, 62, 93-94, 150
Puppy
—common problems 58
—diet 63
—establishing leadership 86
—feeding 63
—first night in new home 52
—health 39, 51, 107
—kindergarten training class
 95
—meeting the family 52
—personality 109
—selection 85, 107
—socialization 53
—teething 59
—temperament 38
—training 54, 56, 85, 96
Puppy-proofing 46, 53
Ra Benji Hassan 13
Rabies 115-116
Racing 105, 144-145

Rawhide 44
Rewards 86, 93, 96, 103
—food 84, 93
Rhabditis **125**
Roaming 116
Robotic dog 25
Rope toys 44
Roundworm 124
Routine 92
Safety 42, 46, 49, 67, 89-90,
 101
—outdoors 50
—yard 153
Sarcoptes mite **121**
Scent attraction 92
Schedule 90, 92
Scolding 18
Seizures 24
Senior dog 111
—diet 66
—health 111
Sensitivity 23, 85
Seoane, Colonel and Mrs. 14,
 15
Separation Anxiety 150-153
Serandida's Only at Sunrise **133**
Shyness 147
Sighthounds 11
Sit 96
Sit/stay 99
Size 22
Skull 21
Socialization 53-54, 56, 84, 96,
 109, 148, 151
Soft toys 44
Spain 15
Spaying 51, 109, 116-117
Sporting dogs 105
Stay 99, 102-103
Stealing food 155
Stray dog 80
Supervision 57, 59, 91
Surgery 117
Taenia pisiformis **126**
Tail 21, 22
Tallaway's Castanet of Loki 16
Tapeworm **125**, **126**
Tassili caves 8
Tattoo 81
Teeth 21, 76-78, 109
Teething period 59
Temperament 38, 147
—evaluation 109
Temperature, taking your dog's
 111
Territorial aggression 149
Testicular cancer 116
Therapy dog 105

Thirst 68
Ticks **120**, **121**
Timing 91, 96, 101, 146
Titian kennels 17
Toxins 50, 67
Toys 43-44, 59, 89-90
Tracking 105, 141-142
Training 83
—basic commands 96-103
—basic principles of 85, 96
—consistent 55, 60
—early 56
—getting started 94
—importance of timing in 91,
 101, 146
—puppy 54, 96
—tips 57
Travel 42
Treats 52, 65, 84, 86, 93, 96
—weaning off in training 103
Tricks 105
Tufford, Beverly 17
Unilateral cryptorchidism 25
United Kennel Club 129
United States 15
Urine marking 116
Vaccinations 51, 54, 109, 114,
 116
Veterinarian 43, 45, 51, 109, 111,
 113, 147
—selection of 112
Veterinary insurance 113
Walker, Helen Whitehouse 137
Water 69, 89
—bowls 41
—increased intake 68
Weight 12, 22
Weir, Mary Jane 17
West of England Ladies Kennel
 Society 14
Westminster Kennel Club 16,
 130
Whining 53, 61, 90
Yard 50

My Ibizan Hound

PUT YOUR PUPPY'S FIRST PICTURE HERE

Dog's Name _____

Date _____ Photographer _____